Help Me! Guide to iOS 1

D1119186

By Charles Hughes

Table of Contents

What's New in iOS 10? 11

1. Managing and Using Widgets 12
2. Using the Lock Screen Widgets 12
3. Using Interactive Notifications 12
4. Unlocking Your iOS 10 Device 13
5. Using Raise to Wake (iPhone 6S and Later Only) 13
6. Reading Transcriptions of Your Voicemails (iPhone Only) 13
7. Using Facial Recognition in Photos 13
8. Viewing Memories in Photos 13
9. Marking Up Photos 14
10. Viewing Related Photos 14
11. Using the New Contacts Application 14
12. Using the New Control Center 14
13. Managing Tabs in Safari 14
14. Using Side-by-Side in Safari 14
15. Viewing a Video on a Webpage while Continuing to Browse 15
16. Handwriting in iMessage 15
17. Previewing a Link Image in a Message 15
18. Sending a Digital Touch in a Message 15
19. Downloading and Using iMessage Applications 15
20. Typing in Multiple Languages at Once 15
21. Using Keyboard Predictions 16
22. Using Tapback in a Message 16

23. Sending a Hidden Text or Photo in a
Message (iPhone 6S and Later Only)................................. 16

24. Using Side-by-Side to Multitask with Mail 16

25. Viewing Three Panes in the Mail Application (iPad Pro Only) 17

26. Unsubscribing from a Mailing List 17

27. Viewing Categories in the App Store 17

28. Using the Music Application....................................... 17

29. Using Side-by-Side to Multitask with Music 17

30. Using 3D Touch to Share an Application.......................... 18

31. Viewing Widgets on the Home Screen
Using 3D Touch (iPhone 6S and Later Only) 18

32. Renaming a Folder Using 3D
Touch (iPhone 6S and Later Only) 18

33. Pausing, Resuming, or Cancelling a Download Using
3D Touch (iPhone 6S and Later Only) 18

34. Showing a Notification within a Folder
Using 3D Touch (iPhone 6S and Later Only) 19

35. Playing Music while Taking Live
Photos (iPhone 6S and Later Only)............................... 19

36. Correcting Siri Queries... 19

37. Adjusting Mail, Contacts, and Calendar Settings Separately 19

38. Searching the Device while Using Any Application 19

39. Removing System Application Icons 20

40. Adjusting Live Photos (iPhone 6S and Later Only) 20

41. Viewing Lyrics in the Music Application........................... 20

42. Viewing Emails in Conversation View 20

43. Turning Read Receipts for a Single Conversation On or Off........ 20

44. Using 3D Touch in the Control
Center (iPhone 6S and Later Only) 21

Getting Started 22

1. Is My Device Compatible with iOS 10? 22

2. Button Layout 23

3. Charging the Device 27

4. Turning the Device On and Off..................................... 28

5. Installing a SIM Card (iPhone and iPad 4G models only)............ 28

6. Setting Up the Device for the First Time.................................. 30

7. Navigating the Screens 38

8. Organizing Icons.. 39

9. Creating an Icon Folder.. 39

10. Using Wi-Fi.. 40

11. Accessing Quick Settings through the Control Center............... 44

12. Using the Notification Center 47

13. Searching the Device for Content 48

14. Managing and Using Widgets.. 48

15. Using Interactive Notifications 51

Making Voice and Video Calls 52

1. Dialing a Number 52

2. Calling a Contact 53

3. Calling a Favorite 55

4. Returning a Recent Phone Call 57

5. Receiving a Voice Call... 58

6. Replying to an Incoming Call with a Text Message 60

7. Setting a Reminder to Return an Incoming Call 61

8. Using the Speakerphone During a Voice Call 61

9. Using the Keypad During a Voice Call... 62

10. Using the Mute Function During a Voice Call 63

11. Putting a Caller on Hold (hidden button)................................... 63

12. Starting a Conference Call (Adding a Call).................................. 63

13. Making a Call Over Wi-Fi.. 64

14. Starting a Facetime Call 67

Managing Contacts.. 69

1. Adding a New Contact... 69

2. Finding a Contact 70

3. Deleting a Contact 72

4. Editing Contact Information 73

5. Sharing a Contact's Information 74

6. Changing the Contact Sort Order.. 77

Text Messaging 81

   1. Composing a New Text Message 81

   2. Copying, Cutting, and Pasting Text 85

   3. Using the Spell Check Feature 87

   4. Receiving a Text Message 88

   5. Reading a Stored Text Message 92

   6. Forwarding a Text Message 92

   7. Calling the Sender from within a Text (iPhone Only) 94

   8. Viewing Sender Information from within a Text 96

   9. Deleting a Text Message 96

   10. Adding Texted Phone Numbers to the Phonebook 97

   11. Sending a Picture Message 99

   12. Leaving a Group Conversation 103

   13. Naming a Conversation 104

   14. Adding a Voice Message to a Conversation (iMessage Only) 104

   15. Sharing Your Location in a Conversation 105

   16. Viewing All Attachments in a Conversation 107

   17. Handwriting a Message 110

   18. Sending a Digital Touch 111

   19. Using Tapback in a Message 111

   20. Turning Read Receipts for a Single Conversation On or Off 112

   21. Using iMessage Applications 112

Using the Safari Web Browser 114

   1. Navigating to a Website 114

   2. Adding and Viewing Bookmarks 115

   3. Adding a Bookmark to the Home Screen 118

   4. Managing Open Browser Tabs 119

   5. Blocking Pop-Up Windows 121

   6. Changing the Search Engine 122

   7. Clearing the History and Browsing Data 123

   8. Viewing an Article in Reader Mode 123

   9. Turning Private Browsing On or Off 125

   10. Setting Up the AutoFill Feature 126

   11. Customizing the Smart Search Field................................. 127

12. Viewing Recently Closed Tabs 128

13. Scanning a Credit Card Using the Device's Camera 129

Managing Photos and Videos 130

1. Taking a Picture 130

2. Capturing a Video 131

3. Using the Digital Zoom 132

4. Using the Flash (iPhone Only) 132

5. Focusing on a Part of the Screen 133

6. Browsing Photos 133

7. Editing a Photo 134

8. Deleting a Photo 138

9. Creating a Photo Album 139

10. Editing a Photo Album 140

11. Deleting a Photo Album 142

12. Starting a Slideshow 142

13. Browsing Photos by Date and Location 143

14. Searching for a Photo 144

15. Recording a Time-Lapse Video 145

16. Recovering Deleted Photos 145

17. Using a Video Overlay to Watch a
Video (Certain iPad Models Only) 146

18. Managing People in Photos 148

19. Managing Memories in Photos 149

20. Capturing and Viewing a Live Photo (iPhone 6S and Later Only) 150

Using iTunes 152

1. Registering with Apple 152

2. Buying Music and Ringtones in iTunes 152

3. Buying or Renting Videos in iTunes 153

4. Searching for Media in iTunes 155

5. Playing Media 156

6. Sharing Your iTunes Account with Family 156

Using the Music Application **158**

1. Downloading Media 158
2. Playing Music 158
3. Using Additional Audio Controls 161
4. Creating a Playlist 162
5. Using the iTunes Radio 165

Using the Mail Application **167**

1. Setting Up the Mail application 167
2. Reading Email 171
3. Switching Accounts in the Mail application 172
4. Writing an Email 173
5. Referring to Another Email when Composing a New Message 174
6. Formatting Text 175
7. Replying to and Forwarding Email Messages 177
8. Attaching a Picture or Video to an Email 178
9. Moving an Email in the Inbox to Another Folder 181
10. Flagging an Important Email 182
11. Archiving Emails 183
12. Changing the Default Signature 184
13. Changing Email Options 185
15. Unsubscribing from an Email List 185
16. Viewing Emails in Conversation View 186

Managing Applications **188**

1. Signing In to an iTunes Account 188
2. Signing In to a Different iTunes Account 190
3. Editing iTunes Account Information 191
4. Searching for an Application to Purchase 192
5. Buying an Application 196
6. Using Wi-Fi to Download an Application 197
7. Switching Between Applications 197
8. Closing an Application Running in the Background 199
9. Organizing Applications into Folders 199
10. Reading User Reviews 199

11. Changing Application Settings 199

12. Deleting an Application 200

13. Sending an Application as a Gift 200

14. Redeeming a Gifted Application 203

15. Turning Automatic Application Updates On or Off..................... 204

16. Using Slide Over to Multitask (Certain iPad Models Only) 204

17. Using Side-by-Side to Multitask (iPad Air 2 and Later Only) 208

Using Siri 209

1. Making a Call Using Siri 209

2. Sending and Receiving Text Messages Using Siri 210

3. Managing the Address Book Using Siri...................................... 210

4. Setting Up and Managing Meetings Using Siri............................ 211

5. Checking the Time and Setting Alarms Using Siri........................ 211

6. Sending and Receiving Email Using Siri 212

7. Getting Directions and Finding Businesses Using Siri.................. 212

8. Playing Music Using Siri 213

9. Searching the Web and Asking Questions Using Siri 213

10. Looking Up Words in the Dictionary Using Siri 214

11. Application-Specific Phrases for Siri.. 214

Adjusting Wireless Settings 215

1. Turning Airplane Mode On or Off.. 215

2. Turning Location Services On or Off... 216

3. Customizing Cellular Data Usage (iPhone and iPad 4G only) 218

4. Turning Data Roaming On or Off (iPhone and iPad 4G only) 220

5. Setting Up a Virtual Private Network (VPN).................................. 220

6. Turning Bluetooth On or Off... 223

7. Using Wi-Fi to Sync Your Device with Your Computer 225

Adjusting Sound Settings 227

1. Turning Vibration On or Off (iPhone Only)................................... 227

2. Turning Volume Button Functionality On or Off............................ 229

3. Setting the Default Ringtone 230

4. Customizing Notification and Alert Sounds 231

5. Turning Lock Sounds On or Off.. 231

6. Turning Keyboard Clicks On or Off.. 232

7. Controlling Siri's Voice 232

8. Adjusting Siri Settings 234

Adjusting Language and Keyboard Settings.................................... 235

1. Customizing Spelling and Grammar Settings 235

2. Adding an International Keyboard 237

3. Adding a Keyboard Shortcut 239

4. Changing the Operating System Language 241

5. Changing the Keyboard Layout.. 243

6. Changing the Region Format.. 245

Adjusting General Settings 247

1. Changing Auto-Lock Settings 247

2. Adjusting the Brightness 249

3. Turning Night Shift On or Off.. 250

4. Assigning a Passcode Lock or Fingerprint Lock........................... 251

5. Turning 24-Hour Mode On or Off.. 256

6. Resetting the Home Screen Layout 257

7. Resetting All Settings... 258

8. Erasing and Restoring the Device.. 259

9. Managing Notification Settings 259

10. Changing the Wallpaper... 261

11. Restricting Access to Private Information.................................... 264

12. Turning Raise to Wake On or Off (iPhone 6S and Later Only)..... 266

Adjusting Accessibility Settings 267

1. Managing Vision Accessibility Features.. 267

2. Managing Hearing Accessibility Features 270

3. Turning Guided Access On or Off... 271

4. Managing Physical & Motor Accessibility Features 272

Adjusting Phone Settings (iPhone Only) 274

1. Turning Call Forwarding On or Off.. 274

2. Turning Call Waiting On or Off 277

3. Turning Caller ID On or Off 279

4. Turning the International Assist On or Off 281

5. Blocking Specific Numbers 281

6. Editing Preset Text Message Responses 283

Adjusting Text Message Settings 284

1. Turning iMessage On or Off 284

2. Turning Read Receipts On or Off in iMessage 286

3. Turning 'Send as SMS' On or Off (iPhone Only) 287

4. Turning MMS Messaging On or Off (iPhone Only) 287

5. Turning the Subject Field On or Off 287

6. Turning the Character Count On or Off (iPhone Only) 288

7. Turning Group Messaging On or Off (iPhone Only) 288

8. Setting the Amount of Time to Keep Messages 289

9. Setting the Expiration Time for Audio Messages 290

10. Turning Raise to Listen On or Off (iPhone Only) 291

11. Blocking Unknown Senders 291

Tips and Tricks 293

1. Maximizing Battery Life 294

2. Taking a Screenshot 294

3. Scrolling to the Top of a Screen 295

4. Saving an Image While Browsing the Internet 295

5. Inserting a Period 295

6. Adding an Extension to a Contact's Number (iPhone only) 295

7. Navigating the Home Screens 295

8. Typing Alternate Characters 295

9. Quickly Deleting Recently Typed Text 296

10. Resetting the Device 296

11. Calling a Phone Number on a Website 296

12. Taking Notes 296

13. Recovering Signal After Being in an Area with No Service 297

14. Changing the Number of Rings Before
    the Device Goes to Voicemail (iPhone only) 297

15. Deleting a Song in the Music Application 298

16. Taking a Picture from the Lock Screen 298

17. Assigning a Custom Ringtone to a Contact 298

18. Opening the Photos Application without Closing the Camera 299

19. Inserting Emoticons 299

20. Hiding the Keyboard in the Messages Application 299

21. Controlling Web Surfing Using Gestures 300

22. Navigating the Menus Using Gestures 300

23. Pausing or Cancelling an Application Download 300

24. Making a Quick Note for a Contact 300

25. Using a Search Engine that Does Not Track Your Searches 301

26. Preventing Applications from Refreshing in the Background 301

27. Leaving Your Home Screen Free of Icons 301

28. Call Waiting in FaceTime 301

29. Viewing Battery Usage 302

30. Attaching Any File Type to an Email 302

31. Viewing Favorite Contacts Using 3D Touch 302

32. Moving the Text Cursor Like a Computer Mouse 302

33. Saving Data by Sending Smaller Pictures 302

34. Filtering Email to Customize Your Inbox 303

35. Using 3D Touch in the Control
    Center (iPhone 6S and Later Only) 303

Troubleshooting 304

1. Device does not turn on 304

2. Device is not responding 305

3. Can't make a call (iPhone Only) 305

4. Can't surf the web 306

5. Screen or keyboard does not rotate 306

6. iTunes does not detect device when connected to a computer 307

7. Device does not ring or play music,
   can't hear while talking, can't listen to voicemails 307

8. Low microphone volume, caller can't hear you (iPhone only) 307

9. Camera does not work 307

10. Device shows the White Screen of Death 308

11. "DEVICE needs to cool down" message appears 308

12. Display does not adjust brightness automatically 309

Index 310

Other Books from the Author of the Help Me Series, Charles Hughes . 314

What's New in iOS 10?

Table of Contents

1. Managing and Using Widgets
2. Using the Lock Screen Widgets
3. Using Interactive Notifications
4. Unlocking Your iOS 10 Device
5. Using Raise to Wake (iPhone 6S and Later Only)
6. Reading Transcriptions of Your Voicemails (iPhone Only)
7. Using Facial Recognition in Photos
8. Viewing Memories in Photos
9. Marking Up Photos
10. Viewing Related Photos
11. Using the New Contacts Application
12. Using the New Control Center
13. Managing Tabs in Safari
14. Using Side-by-Side in Safari
15. Viewing a Video on a Webpage while Continuing to Browse
16. Handwriting in iMessage
17. Previewing a Link Image in a Message
18. Sending a Digital Touch in a Message
19. Using iMessage Applications
20. Typing in Multiple Languages at Once
21. Using Keyboard Predictions
22. Using Tapback in a Message
23. Sending a Hidden Text or Photo in a Message (iPhone 6S and Later Only
24. Using Side-by-Side to Multitask with Mail
25. Viewing Three Panes in the Mail Application (iPad Pro Only)
26. Unsubscribing from a Mailing List
27. Viewing Categories in the App Store
28. Using the Music Application
29. Using Side-by-Side to Multitask with Music
30. Using 3D Touch to Share an Application
31. Viewing Widgets on the Home Screen Using 3D Touch (iPhone 6S and Later Only)
32. Renaming a Folder Using 3D Touch (iPhone 6S and Later Only)
33. Pausing, Resuming, or Cancelling a Download Using 3D Touch (iPhone 6S and Later Only)
34. Showing a Notification within a Folder Using 3D Touch (iPhone 6S and Later Only)
35. Playing Music while Taking Live Photos (iPhone 6S and Later Only)

36. Correcting Siri Queries
37. Adjusting Mail, Contacts, and Calendar Settings Separately
38. Searching the Device while Using Any Application
39. Removing System Application Icons
40. Adjusting Live Photos (iPhone 6S and Later Only)
41. Viewing Lyrics in the Music Application
42. Viewing Emails in Conversation View
43. Turning Read Receipts for a Single Conversation On or Off
44. Using 3D Touch in the Control Center (iPhone 6S and Later Only)

1. Managing and Using Widgets

You can now use widgets that allow you to access information within applications more quickly, such as photo memories, calendar, music, and many more. To view the current widgets, touch the top of the screen and slide your finger down at any time, even when using an application. Slide your finger to the right to view the widgets. You can also access widgets by sliding your finger to the right when you are on the main Home screen. Refer to *"Managing and Using Widgets"* on page 48 to learn more.

2. Using the Lock Screen Widgets

Widgets are also accessible directly from the Home screen. Without unlocking your device, slide your finger to the right to view the available widgets. You can also search the iPad directly from the lock screen. Refer to *"Managing and Using Widgets"* on page 48 to learn more.

3. Using Interactive Notifications

When a notification arrives on the lock screen, you can now view it or clear it immediately. When a message notification arrives while the device is unlocked, you can reply to the message from the notification and attach images or audio. Refer to *"Using Interactive Notifications"* on page 51 to learn more.

4. Unlocking Your iOS 10 Device

Since the lock screen now contains widgets, you can no longer slide to the right to unlock your device. Instead, press the Home button when the lock screen is visible to unlock.

5. Using Raise to Wake (iPhone 6S and Later Only)

iOS 10 on the iPhone allows you to activate the screen without pressing any buttons. Turn on the Raise to Wake feature and pick up the phone to activate the screen. Refer to *"Turning Raise to Wake On or Off"* on page 266 to learn more.

6. Reading Transcriptions of Your Voicemails (iPhone Only)

iOS 10 on the iPhone automatically transcribes your voicemails, allowing you to read your voicemails as text. To read a voicemail transcription touch the voicemail on the Voicemail screen in the Phone application. To open the Voicemail screen, touch **Voicemail** in the Phone application.

7. Using Facial Recognition in Photos

Photos now recognizes faces to place groups of photos in the same folder when they contain the same person. The Memories folder also uses the facial recognition feature to create photo arrangements. Refer to *"Managing People in Photos"* on page 148 to learn more about grouping photos with the same person in a folder.

8. Viewing Memories in Photos

Your device now creates photo arrangements, called Memories, based on the people in the photo and the location. This is an automatic feature. Refer to *"Managing Memories in Photos"* on page 149 to learn more.

9. Marking Up Photos

You can now draw on photos, add text, and add additional effects to photos. Refer to *"Editing a Photo"* on page 134 to learn more.

10. Viewing Related Photos

If a photo contains the same people or was taken in the same location or on the same date as others, you can view the related photos by touching the photo and sliding your finger up.

11. Using the New Contacts Application

The Contacts application has been redesigned. Refer to *"Managing Contacts"* on page 69 to learn how to use it.

12. Using the New Control Center

The Control Center is now easier to access and has additional features. Touch the bottom of the screen and slide your finger up to immediately open the Control Center. Refer to *"Accessing Quick Settings through the Control Center"* on page 44 to learn more.

13. Managing Tabs in Safari

Safari now allows you to open as many tabs as you like. You can also open and close tabs more easily. Refer to *"Managing Open Browser Tabs"* on page 119 to learn more.

14. Using Side-by-Side in Safari

You can now view two tabs at the same time in Split-Screen mode in Safari. Refer to *"Managing Open Browser Tabs"* on page 119 to learn more.

15. Viewing a Video on a Webpage while Continuing to Browse

Safari now lets you start a video on a webpage and leave it playing while you continue to browse the webpage. You can also navigate to another tab and the video will continue to play. If you lock your device, the video pauses. When you unlock your device again, the video automatically resumes.

16. Handwriting in iMessage

Send a handwritten message when using iMessage, which plays animated handwriting on the recipient's screen. Refer to *"Handwriting a Message"* on page 110 to learn more.

17. Previewing a Link Image in a Message

When you send a link to an image in iMessage, a small preview of the image now appears right in the conversation.

18. Sending a Digital Touch in a Message

You can now send a heartbeat or tap sequence in a message. This types of message is called Digital Touch. Refer to *"Sending a Digital Touch"* on page 111 to learn how.

19. Downloading and Using iMessage Applications

There are certain applications that can now interact with iMessage. Each iMessage application in the App Store is indicated by the label "Offers iMessage App'. Refer to *"Using iMessage Applications"* on page 112 to learn more.

20. Typing in Multiple Languages at Once

If you start typing in English and then wish to insert one or more words in another language, iOS 10 will now suggest words in foreign languages.

21. Using Keyboard Predictions

Keyboard predictions have been drastically improved in iOS 10. Your device will now recognize common phrases and text that you have typed before to suggest words, which appear above the keyboard as you type.

22. Using Tapback in a Message

When you receive a message in iMessage, you can immediately respond with an emoji that appears directly on the person's original message. For example, you can send a thumbs up or a heart that appears on the original message. This feature is compatible with any type of message, be it text, image, Digital Touch, or anything else. Refer to *"Using Tapback in a Message"* on page 113 to learn more.

23. Sending a Hidden Text or Photo in a Message (iPhone 6S and Later Only)

You can now send text messages and photos that are invisible (shrouded in white mist) until they are touched. This feature is called Invisible Ink. To send an Invisible Ink message, type your

message or attach a photo, then 3D Touch (firmly press) the button. A list of options

appears. Touch Invisible Ink, then touch the button again.

24. Using Side-by-Side to Multitask with Mail

Mail is now compatible with side-by-side multitasking, allowing you to use Mail and a second application at the same time. Refer to *"Using Side-by-Side to Multitask"* on page 114 to learn more.

25. Viewing Three Panes in the Mail Application (iPad Pro Only)

iOS 10 on the iPad Pro allows you to simultaneously view a list of your mailboxes, the mailbox contents of the mailbox that is currently selected, and the contents of the message that is currently selected. To do this, rotate your iPad Pro horizontally and touch the ⊟ button to the left of 'Mailboxes'.

26. Unsubscribing from a Mailing List

You can now unsubscribe from lists that crowd your inbox with unwanted emails. Refer to *"Unsubscribing from an Email List"* on page 186 to learn more.

27. Viewing Categories in the App Store

In iOS 9, the ability to browse applications by category in the App store was eliminated. iOS 10 brings back this functionality. Refer to *"Searching for an Application to Purchase"* on page 192 to learn more.

28. Using the Music Application

The Music application has been completely redesigned in iOS 10. Refer to *"Using the Music Application"* on page 158 to learn more.

29. Using Side-by-Side to Multitask with Music

Music is now compatible with side-by-side multitasking, allowing you to use Music and a second application at the same time. Refer to *"Using Side-by-Side to Multitask"* on page 208 to learn more.

30. Using 3D Touch to Share an Application

If you have downloaded an application from the App Store, you can share a link to the application by 3D Touching (firmly pressing) the application on your Home screen. Then, touch **Share APPNAME**, where APPNAME stands for the name of the application. A list of sharing options appear.

31. Viewing Widgets on the Home Screen Using 3D Touch (iPhone 6S and Later Only)

If an application has a corresponding widget, such as Weather or News, you can 3D Touch (firmly press) the application icon on the Home screen to see its widget. Touch the widget to open the application.

32. Renaming a Folder Using 3D Touch (iPhone 6S and Later Only)

You can now quickly rename a folder by 3D Touching (firmly pressing) it. Touch **Rename** when the folder options appear. Refer to *"Creating an Icon Folder"* on page 39 to learn more about folders.

33. Pausing, Resuming, or Cancelling a Download Using 3D Touch (iPhone 6S and Later Only)

When downloading an application from the App Store, you can now pause it, resume the download, or cancel the download by 3D Touching (firmly pressing) the application icon. Touch one of the options that appears after 3D Touching the icon.

34. Showing a Notification within a Folder Using 3D Touch (iPhone 6S and Later Only)

If an application within a folder has one or more notifications, you can 3D Touch (firmly press) the folder to view the applications with notifications. Touch the name of the application to open it.

35. Playing Music while Taking Live Photos (iPhone 6S and Later Only)

You can now capture live photos while listening to music. Refer to *"Capturing and Viewing a Live Photo"* on page 150 to learn how to capture a live photo.

36. Correcting Siri Queries

When you misspeak or Siri does not hear you correctly, you can fix the query by touching the text at the top of the screen. A list of suggestions appears under 'Maybe you said'. Touch a suggestion to have Siri search again. Refer to *"Using Siri"* on page 209 to learn more.

37. Adjusting Mail, Contacts, and Calendar Settings Separately

Prior to iOS 10, Mail, Contacts, and Calendar settings could be adjusted from the same screen in Settings. In iOS 10, they have been separated into their own tabs. Refer to *"Using the Mail Application"* on page 167 and *"Managing Contacts"* on page 69 to learn more about adjusting these settings.

38. Searching the Device while Using Any Application

You can now use spotlight search to search the iPad, the App store, the web, and even content within applications at any time. This feature is even available while using an application. A Search field has been added to the Notification center. Refer to *"Using the Notification Center"* on page 47 to learn more.

39. Removing System Application Icons

You can now remove certain applications icons for applications that come with your device, such as Music or FaceTime. Removing an application icon for system applications does not delete them. You can always bring back the icon by searching for the application in the App Store. Refer to *"Deleting an Application"* on page 200 to learn more.

40. Adjusting Live Photos (iPhone 6S and Later Only)

You can now edit Live photos just as you would any other photo. To edit a Live photo, touch the button at the bottom of the screen. Refer to *"Editing a Photo"* on page 134 to learn more.

41. Viewing Lyrics in the Music Application

You can now view lyrics for a song that is currently playing in the Music application. To view the lyrics, touch **Lyrics** while a song is playing. If you do not see the Lyrics option, touch the album cover in the lower right-hand corner of the screen.

42. Viewing Emails in Conversation View

The Mail application now lets you view email threads, or a list of emails that you have exchanged with a single contact or group. Refer to *"Viewing Emails in Conversation View"* on page 186 to learn more.

43. Turning Read Receipts for a Single Conversation On or Off

Whenever you send a message in iMessage, you receive a confirmation when the recipient reads the message. Before iOS 10, you could only turn Read Receipts on or off for all iMessage conversations. In iOS 10, you can adjust the same setting for each conversation. Refer to *"Turning Read Receipts for a Single Conversation On or Off"* on page 112 to learn more.

44. Using 3D Touch in the Control Center (iPhone 6S and Later Only)

You can now use 3D Touch in the Control Center to access additional features. Refer to *"Using 3D Touch in the Control Center"* on page 21 to learn how.

Getting Started

Table of Contents

1. Is My Device Compatible with iOS 10?
2. Button Layout
3. Charging the Device
4. Turning the Device On and Off
5. Installing a SIM Card
6. Setting Up the Device for the First Time
7. Navigating the Screens
8. Organizing Icons
9. Creating an Icon Folder
10. Using Wi-Fi
11. Accessing Quick Settings through the Control Center
12. Using the Notification Center
13. Searching the Device for Content
14. Managing and Using Widgets
15. Using Interactive Notifications

1. Is My Device Compatible with iOS 10?

You can upgrade to iOS 10 if you have one of the following devices:

- iPhone 5
- iPhone 5C
- iPhone 5S
- iPhone SE
- iPhone 6
- iPhone 6 Plus
- iPhone 6S
- iPhone 6S Plus
- iPad 4th generation
- iPad Air
- iPad Air 2
- iPad mini 2
- iPad mini 3

- iPad mini 4
- iPad Pro 9.7-inch
- iPad Pro 12.9-inch
- iPod Touch 6th Generation

2. Button Layout

iOS devices have four buttons and one switch (no switch on the iPad Air 2 and later). The rest of the functionality is controlled by the touchscreen. Each button has several functions, depending on the context in which it is used.

Note: Button locations may vary based on the iOS device.

The buttons perform the following functions, as shown in the iPhone 6 example below:

Home Button

Figure 1: Front View

Home Button
- Shows the Home screen.
- Displays open applications when pressed twice quickly.

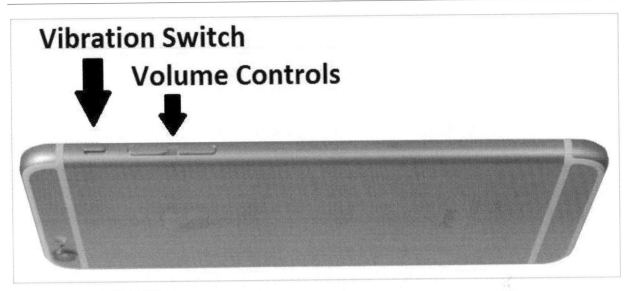

Figure 2: Left Side View

Volume Controls (located on the right side of the device on an iPad)
- Controls the volume of the ringer. Refer to *"Adjusting Sound Settings"* on page 227 to learn more about setting ringtones or the sound volume.
- Controls the volume of the earpiece or speakerphone during a conversation.
- Controls the media volume.

Vibration Switch / Side Switch (located on the right side of the device on an iPad, except for iPad Air 2 and later)

- Turns Vibration on or off on an iPhone
- Turns the Sound on or off, or locks and unlocks the screen rotation on an iPad, depending on the settings.

Headphone Jack

Figure 3: Bottom View

Headphone Jack (at the top of the device on an iPad) - Allows headphones or speakers to be plugged in. Allows an AUX cable to be plugged in to hear the device over the speakers in a car or stereo.

Lightning Connector (iPhone 5, 5S, 6, 6 Plus, iPad Mini, and iPad 4th generation and later) - Connects the device to a computer in order to transfer data. Connects the device to a charger

Figure 4: Right Side View

Sleep/Wake Button (at the top of the device on an iPad)

- Turns the device on and off.
- Locks and unlocks the device

3. Charging the Device

To ensure that the device works well, please follow these guidelines:

Note: You cannot use a cable that came with an iPhone 4S or earlier to charge an iPhone 5 or later. Similarly, you cannot use a cable that came with an iPad 3 (New iPad, released in March 2012) to charge an iPad 4 or later (iPad with Retina Display, released in November 2012).

Discharge the device completely at least once a month for optimal performance. When charging the battery, the meter in the upper right-hand corner of the screen (when unlocked) may show that it is fully charged; however, the charge is not complete until **100% Charged** appears on the lock screen. Insert the Lightning cable into the Lightning Connector on the bottom of the phone. The

lightning cable looks like this: . When the cable is inserted correctly, the indicator sound is played or the device vibrates (vibration on iPhone only). Refer to *"Tips and Tricks"* on page 293 to learn about conserving battery life.

4. Turning the Device On and Off

Use the Sleep/Wake button to turn the device on or off. To turn the device on, press and hold

the **Sleep/Wake** button for two seconds. The device turns on and the logo is displayed. After the device has finished starting up, the Lock screen is displayed.
To unlock the device, press the Home button while the screen is on, or enter your password or fingerprint.

Note: If the device does not turn on after a few seconds, try charging the battery.

To turn the device off, press and hold the **Sleep/Wake** button until the screen becomes dark. The

message "Slide to power off" appears. Touch the slider and move your finger to the right. The device turns off.

*Note: To keep the device on, touch **Cancel** or do not take any action at all.*

5. Installing a SIM Card (iPhone and iPad 4G models only)

Insert the SIM card from an old phone to retain your personal information and phone number. iPhone 5 and later models only take nano SIM cards. The type of SIM card also depends on your carrier. For instance, you cannot insert a Verizon SIM card into an AT&T device, and vice-versa. To install a SIM card:

1. Insert the end of a paper clip or a SIM eject tool into the hole on the right side of the device if it is an iPhone, or on the left side if it is an iPad. The SIM card tray pops out, as shown in **Figure 5**.
2. Take out the old SIM card, if necessary, and insert the new SIM card with the short side facing upwards, as shown in **Figure 6**.
3. Re-insert the tray into the device. The new SIM card is installed.

Note: An iPhone 4S is used as an example in the images below. The SIM card tray on some iOS 10 devices is located on the left side of the device.

Figure 5: SIM Card Tray

Figure 6: SIM Card Inserted

6. Setting Up the Device for the First Time

You must set up the iOS 10 device when you turn it on for the first time, unless an Apple associate or another specialist has already done so for you. To set up the device:

Note: Some steps in the following procedure may not apply to your iOS device.

1. Turn on the device by pressing and holding the **Power** button until the ![icon] icon appears. The device starts up and the Welcome screen appears, as shown in **Figure 7**.
2. Touch the screen anywhere and move your finger to the right to begin setting up your device. The Language screen appears, as shown in **Figure 8**.
3. Touch a language in the list. The language is selected, and the Country screen appears, as shown in **Figure 9**.
4. Touch the country where you reside. The country is selected, and the Wi-Fi Networks screen appears.
5. Touch a Wi-Fi network. The Password prompt appears.
6. Enter the network password, which is usually found on your wireless router. Touch **Join** in the upper right-hand corner of the screen. The device connects to the selected Wi-Fi network and the Location Services screen appears, as shown in **Figure 10**. If you did not activate your device in the store, you may need to confirm your phone number before the Location Services screen appears. Enter your billing zip code and the last four digits of your social security number to confirm (iPhone 6 and iPhone 6 Plus only).
7. Touch **Enable Location Services** if you want to turn the feature on. Touch **Disable Location Services** to leave the feature turned off. Some applications will not work with Location Services turned off. The Set Up device screen appears, as shown in **Figure 11**
8. Touch **Restore from iCloud Backup** or **Restore from iTunes Backup** if you have a data backup. You will need to connect the device to your computer and run iTunes if you touch 'Restore from iTunes Backup'. Touch **Set Up as New device** if you do not have an iCloud or iTunes backup. The Apple ID screen appears.
9. Touch **Sign In with your Apple ID** if you have an Apple ID or touch **Create a Free Apple ID**. The Terms and Conditions screen appears once you are signed in.
10. Touch **Agree** in the bottom right-hand corner of the screen. A confirmation dialog appears.
11. Touch **Agree** again. The iCloud screen appears.
12. Touch **Use iCloud** to use the feature or touch **Don't Use iCloud** to disable it. The Find My device feature (iPhone or iPad) is turned on automatically when you use iCloud. The iMessage and FaceTime screen appears.
13. Touch a phone number or email address if you would like to enable it for iMessage or FaceTime. A blue check mark appears next to each selected address or number.
14. Touch **Next** in the upper right-hand corner of the screen when you are finished. The iCloud drive screen appears. iCloud Drive syncs all of your documents and images in iCloud, and updates them on all of your devices as you work.

15. Touch Upgrade to iCloud Drive. iCloud Drive is turned on, and the Passcode Creation screen appears, as shown in Figure 12.

16. Enter a passcode to set up a security lock for your phone, or touch Don't Add Passcode to do it later. The Display Zoom screen appears, as shown in **Figure 13** (iPhone 6 and 6 Plus and later).

17. Touch the device on the left to view the most amount of information on your screen. However, the fonts will be slightly harder to read. Touch the device on the right to use your device in zoomed view. Fonts will be easier to read, but the screen will not fit as much information. The Diagnostics screen appears.

18. Touch **Automatically Send** to have the device send usage data to Apple or touch **Don't Send** to disable this feature. Usage Data contains anonymous statistics about the ways in which you use your device.

19. Touch **Get Started**. The device setup is complete.

Figure 7: Welcome Screen

Figure 8: Language Screen

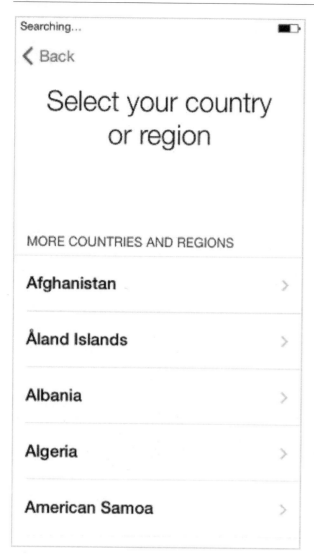

Figure 9: Country Screen

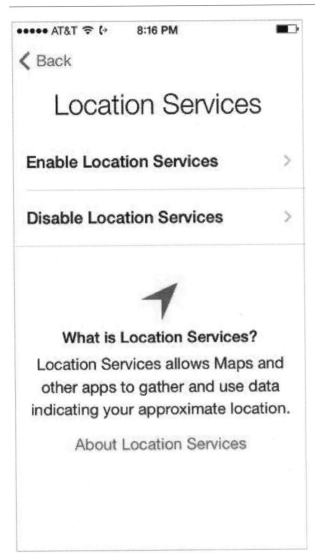

Figure 10: Location Services Screen

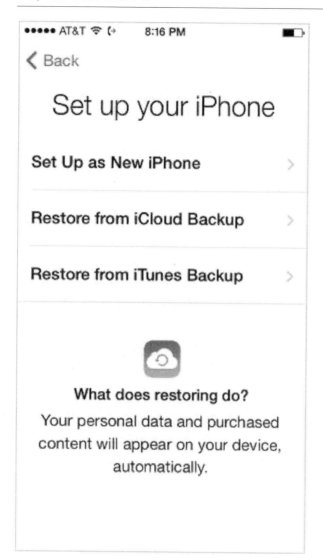

Figure 11: Wi-Fi Networks Screen

Figure 12: Passcode Creation Screen

Figure 13: Display Zoom Screen

7. Navigating the Screens

There are many ways to navigate iOS 10 devices. Use the following tips to quickly navigate the screens of the device:

- Use the **Home** button to return to the Home screen at any time. Any application or tool that you were using will be in the same state when you return to it.
- At the Home screen, slide your finger to the left to access additional pages. If nothing happens, the other pages are blank.

- Touch the center of the Home screen and slide your finger down to access the device's search feature. You may search any data stored on your phone, including application data, as well as the web, iTunes, Application Store, movie show times, locations nearby, and much more. Refer to *"Searching the Device for Content"* on page 48 to learn more.

8. Organizing Icons

You may wish to re-order the location of the application icons on the screens. To organize application icons:

1. Touch an icon and hold it until all of the icons begin to shake. The icons can now be moved around the screen.
2. Move the icon to the desired location and let go of the screen. The icon is relocated and the surrounding icons are re-ordered accordingly. If an icon that used to be on the screen is gone, then it has been moved to a different Home screen in the process.
3. To move an icon to another screen, move the icon to the edge of the current one and hold it there. The adjacent screen appears. Drop the icon in the desired location.
4. Press the **Home** button. The icons stop shaking.

9. Creating an Icon Folder

When there are many icons on the Home screens, you may wish to organize the icons into folders. Each folder can have a meaningful name to enable you to find the icons easily. To create a folder:

1. Touch an icon and hold it until all of the icons begin to shake. The icons can now be moved.
2. Move one icon on top of another and let go of the screen. A folder with the selected icons is created, as shown in **Figure 14**. Touch the ⊗ button to enter a name for the folder.
3. Enter a name for the folder, and touch **Done**. The new name is saved.
4. To exit the folder, touch anywhere outside of it. The folder closes.
5. Press the **Home** button. The icons stop shaking.

Note: To add more icons to a folder, just touch an icon while it is shaking and move it onto the folder.

Figure 14: A New Folder

10. Using Wi-Fi

Use a nearby Wi-Fi hotspot or a home router to avoid having to use data. Wi-Fi is required to download large applications. To turn on Wi-Fi:

1. Touch the ⚙ icon. The Settings screen appears, as shown in **Figure 15**.
2. Touch **Wi-Fi**. The Wi-Fi Networks screen appears, as shown in **Figure 16**.
3. Touch the ⬭ switch next to 'Wi-Fi'. Wi-Fi turns on and a list of available networks appears, as shown in **Figure 17**. If the network has an 🔒 icon next to it, a password is needed to connect to it.
4. Touch the network to which you would like to connect. The Wi-Fi Password prompt appears if the network is protected, as shown in **Figure 18**.
5. Enter the network password. Touch **Join**. Provided that you entered the correct password, a check mark appears next to the network name and the 📶 icon appears at the top of the screen. You are connected to the Wi-Fi network.

Note: If you enter an incorrect password, the message "Unable to join the network >Network Name<" appears, where '>Network Name<' is the name of your network. The network password is usually written on the modem given to you by your internet service provider. It is sometimes called a WEP Key.

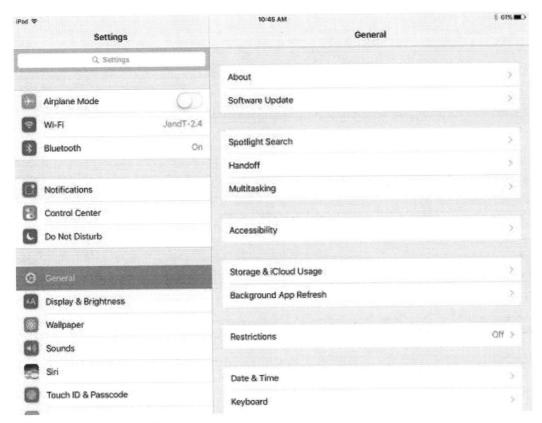

Figure 15: Settings Screen

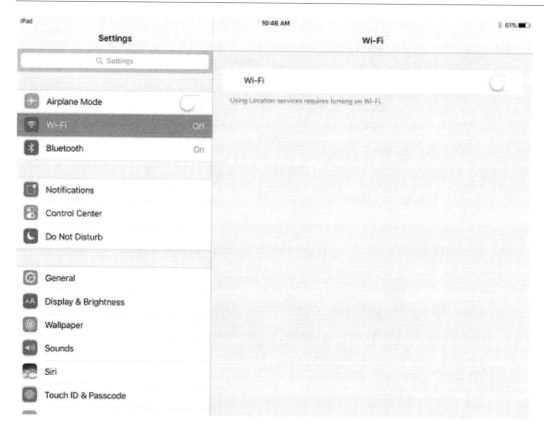

Figure 16: Wi-Fi Networks Screen

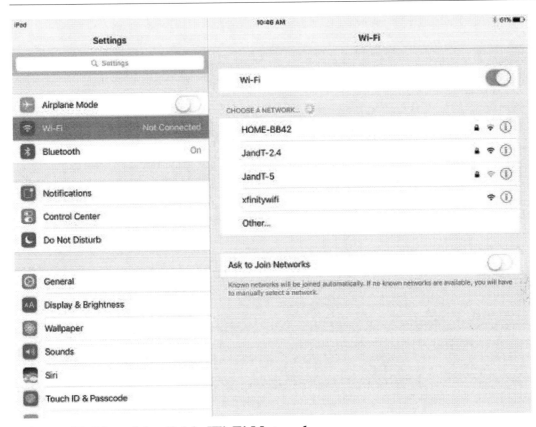

Figure 17: List of Available Wi-Fi Networks

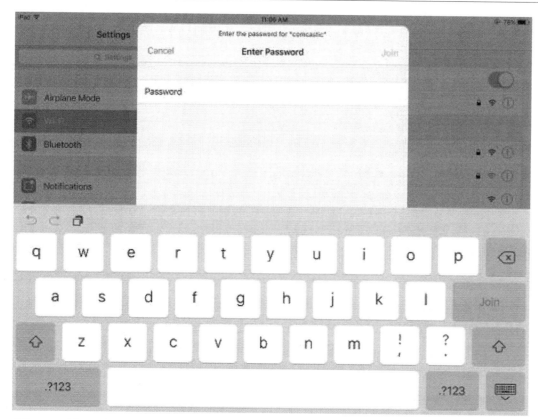

Figure 18: Wi-Fi Password Prompt

11. Accessing Quick Settings through the Control Center

There are various settings that you can access without opening the Settings screen by using the Control Center. To use the Control Center:

1. Touch the bottom of the screen at any time and slide your finger up. The Control Center appears, as shown in **Figure 19**.
2. Touch one of the following icons at the top of the Control Center to turn on the corresponding function:

 \- Turns Airplane mode on or off.

 \- Turns Wi-Fi on or off.

 \- Turns Bluetooth on or off.

 \- Turns 'Do not disturb' on or off.

 \- Turns automatic screen rotation on or off.

- Turns all sounds on or off on an iPad.

A white icon, such as a icon, indicates that the function is turned on.

3. Touch one of the following icons at the bottom of the Control Center to turn on the corresponding service:

 - Turns the flashlight on or off (iPhone only).

 - Opens the timer application.

 - Opens the calculator application (iPhone only).

 - Turns on the camera.

 - Turns Night Shift on or off. Refer to **Turning Night Shift On or Off**

You can also slide your finger to the left to open the Music controls, as shown in **Figure 20**. From this screen, you can control music that is playing. You can also start playing the music on a Bluetooth device connected to your iPhone, iPad, or iPod. Slide your finger to the left again to open the Home controls, which lets you manage your Home accessories quickly.

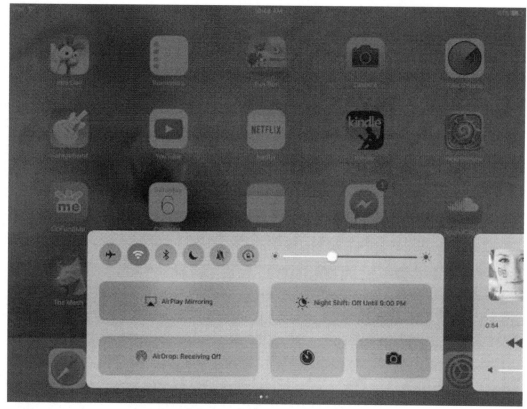

Figure 19: Control Center Main Screen

Figure 20: Music Controls in Control Center

12. Using the Notification Center

The Notification Center shows event reminders and all types of alerts, such as calendar events, received texts, and missed calls. You can also search the iPad, App Store, the web, or even content within applications from this screen.

To open the notification center, touch the top of the screen at any time (even while using an application) and move your finger down. Touch a notification to open the corresponding application. For instance, touch a calendar event to open the calendar. You can also touch **All** or **Missed** at the top of the screen to view the corresponding call notifications.

To perform a search, touch the Search field at the top of the Notification center. Matching results appear as you type.

On the iPhone 6S and later, you can 3D Touch (firmly press) the X icon to clear all notifications at once.

13. Searching the Device for Content

To find an application, email, contact, event, or other item on your device, search the device. To search for content, touch the center of any home screen, and slide your finger down. The Search screen appears. Search results appear as you type. You can also call or message contacts directly from the search results. You can also perform a search *"Using the Notification Center"* on page 47.

14. Managing and Using Widgets

iOS 10 introduced widgets to the iPhone and iPad. A widget is a tool that you can use to quickly find content within applications, such as calendar events, email, and photos. You can use widgets both in the Notification center and on the Lock screen.

To use a widget, open the Notification center and slide your finger to the right. The Widget screen appears, as shown in **Figure 21**.

To manage widgets:

1. Touch **Edit**. The Add Widgets screen appears, as shown in **Figure 22**.
2. Touch the ⊖ icon next to a widget, and then touch **Remove** to remove a widget from the Widget screen.
3. Touch the ⊕ icon next to a widget to add it to the Widget screen.
4. Touch **Done**. The updated Widget screen appears.

You can also view the Widgets screen on the Lock screen by sliding your finger to the right, as shown in **Figure 23**.

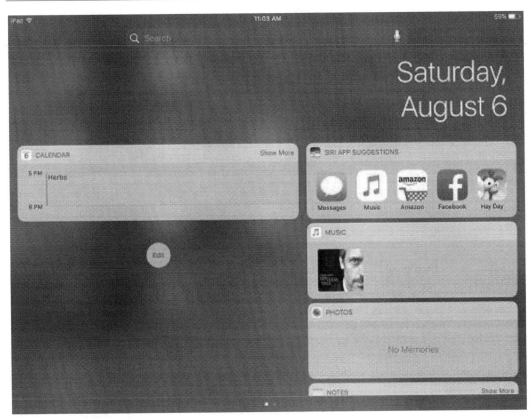

Figure 21: Widget Screen in the Notification Center

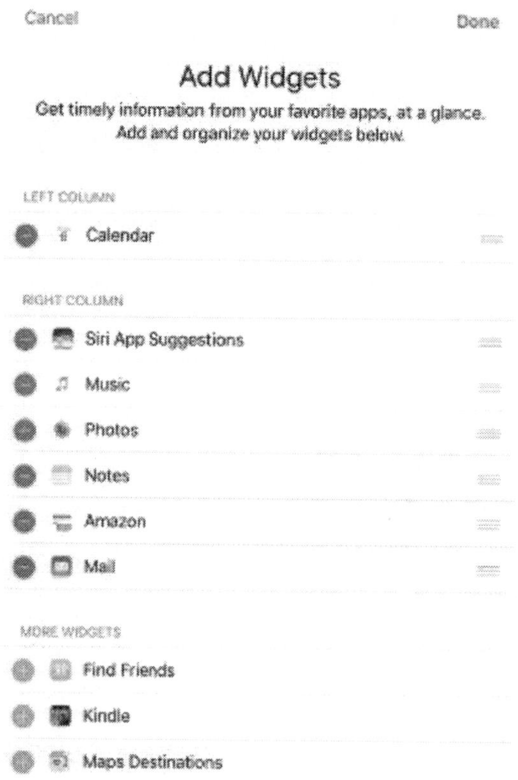

Cancel   Done

Add Widgets

Get timely information from your favorite apps, at a glance.
Add and organize your widgets below.

LEFT COLUMN

● 🎂 Calendar

RIGHT COLUMN

● 📺 Siri App Suggestions

● 🎵 Music

● 🌸 Photos

● 📝 Notes

● 🛒 Amazon

● 📧 Mail

MORE WIDGETS

● 🔲 Find Friends

● 📱 Kindle

● 🗺️ Maps Destinations

Figure 22: Add Widgets Screen

Figure 23: Widget Screen on the Lock Screen

15. Using Interactive Notifications

When a notification arrives on the lock screen, you can view it or clear it immediately. When a message notification arrives while the device is unlocked, you can reply to the message from the notification and attach images or audio. Use the following tips with interactive notifications:

- Slide your finger to the left to view the notification options. Touch **Clear** or **View** to perform the associated action.
- Slide your finger to the right to view the notification. On an iPhone, sliding your finger to the right on a Missed Call notification immediately returns the call.
- (iPhone 6S and later only) Firmly touch (3D Touch) the Missed Call notification to return the call or
- (iPhone 6S and later only) Firmly touch (3D Touch) the text message notification to quickly reply to the text.

Making Voice and Video Calls

Sections 1-13 below only apply to an iPhone running iOS 10. Section 14 applies to both iPhone and iPad.

Table of Contents

1. Dialing a Number
2. Calling a Contact
3. Calling a Favorite
4. Returning a Recent Phone Call
5. Receiving a Voice Call
6. Replying to an Incoming Call with a Text Message
7. Setting a Reminder to Return an Incoming Call
8. Using the Speakerphone During a Voice Call
9. Using the Keypad During a Voice Call
10. Using the Mute Function During a Voice Call
11. Putting a Caller on Hold (hidden button)
12. Starting a Conference Call (Adding a Call)
13. Making a Call Over Wi-Fi
14. Starting a Facetime Call

1. Dialing a Number

Numbers that are not in your Phonebook can be dialed on the keypad. To manually dial a phone number, touch the [icon] icon on the Home screen. The keypad appears, as shown in **Figure 1**. Touch the [icon] icon at the bottom of the screen, if you do not see the keypad. Enter the desired phone number and then touch the [icon] at the bottom of the screen. The device dials the number.

Figure 1: Keypad

2. Calling a Contact

If a number is stored in your Phonebook, you may touch the name of a contact to dial it. To call a contact already stored in your device:

1. Touch the ![icon] icon on the Home screen. The Phonebook appears, as shown in **Figure 2**.
2. Touch the name of a contact. The Contact Information screen appears, as shown in **Figure 3**.
3. Touch the desired phone number. The device calls the contact's number. Refer to *"Managing Contacts"* on page 69 to learn more about adding or removing contacts.

Note: For some unexplained reason, Apple has decided to place the ![icon] icon in the Extras folder by default. If you cannot find it, look in that folder.

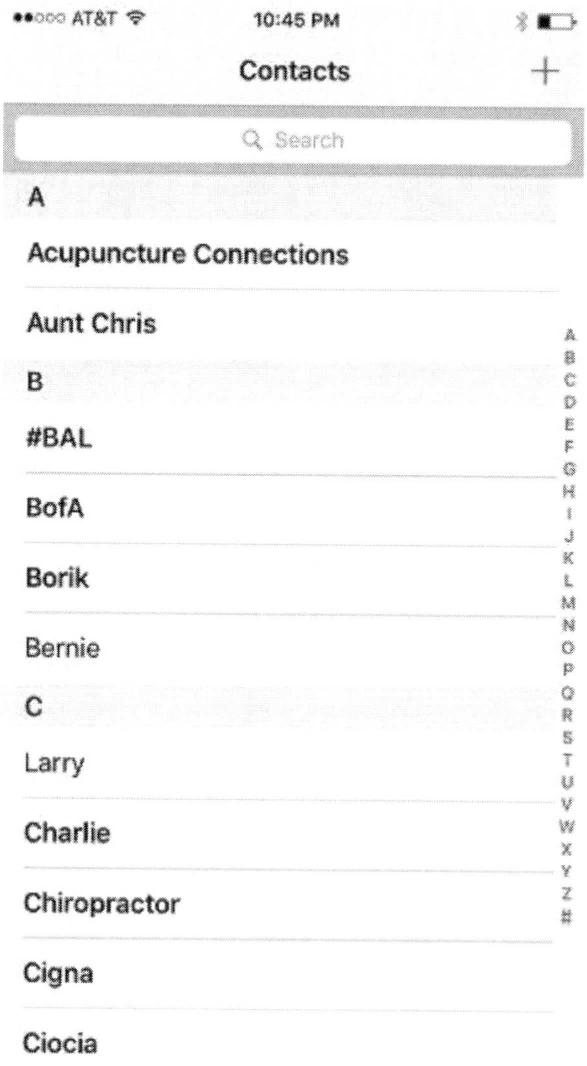

●●○○○ AT&T 📶   10:45 PM   ⁕ ▬▭

Contacts   +

🔍 Search

A

Acupuncture Connections

Aunt Chris

B

#BAL

BofA

Borik

Bernie

C

Larry

Charlie

Chiropractor

Cigna

Ciocia

A
B
C
D
E
F
G
H
I
J
K
L
M
N
O
P
Q
R
S
T
U
V
W
X
Y
Z
#

Figure 2: Phonebook

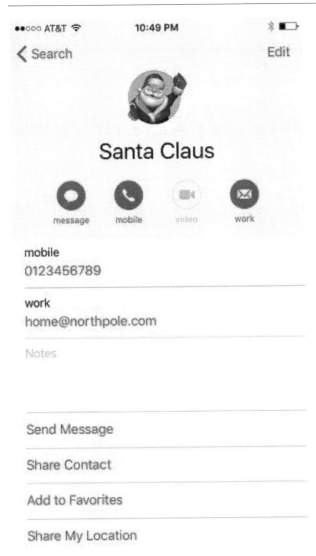

Figure 3: Contact Information Screen

3. Calling a Favorite

There is no Speed Dial feature on iPhones with iOS 10. Instead, frequently dialed numbers can be saved as Favorites, which can be accessed more quickly than other contacts. To call a number stored in Favorites:

1. Touch the 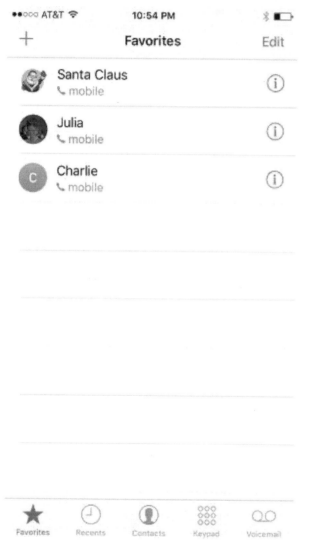 icon on the Home screen. The keypad screen appears.
2. Touch the ☆ icon at the bottom of the screen. The Favorites screen appears, as shown in **Figure 4**. If you wish to add a Favorite contact, touch the ＋ button.
3. Touch the name of a Favorite. The device calls the selected number. Refer to *"Managing Contacts"* on page 69 to learn more about managing Favorites.

Figure 4: Favorites Screen

4. Returning a Recent Phone Call

After missing a call, your device will notify you of who called and at what time. The device also shows a history of all recently placed calls. To view and return a missed call or redial a recently entered number:

1. Touch the ![phone icon] icon on the Home screen. The Calling screen appears.

2. Touch the ![clock icon] icon at the bottom of the screen. The Recent Calls screen appears, with the most recent calls on top. Missed or declined calls are shown in red. The ![call icon] icon is shown next to a placed call, as shown in **Figure 5**.

3. Touch the name of a contact. The device dials the contact.

You can also return a missed call by touching the notification on the Lock screen and sliding your finger to the right. Refer to *"Using Interactive Notifications"* on page 51 to learn more.

*Note: To view only missed calls, touch **missed** at the top of the Recent Calls screen.*

Figure 5: Recent Calls Screen

5. Receiving a Voice Call

There are several ways to accept or reject a voice call based on whether or not the screen is locked. Use the following tips when receiving a voice call:

- To receive an incoming voice call while the device is locked, touch and move the 📞 on the slider to the right, as shown in **Figure 6**. The call is answered.
- To mute the ringer, press the Sleep/Wake button. To reject the incoming call, press the Sleep/Wake button again.

- To receive an incoming call while using an application (or viewing a Home screen), touch the button, as shown in **Figure 7**. To reject the incoming call, touch the button. The call is declined. The number then appears in red in the list of recent calls, signifying that it is a missed call, and a notification appears above the icon on the Home screen.

- Touch **Message** or **Remind Me** to decline a call if you are currently busy but wish to address it later. Refer to *"Replying to an Incoming Call with a Text Message"* on page 60 or *"Setting a Reminder to Return an Incoming Call"* on page 61 to learn more about these options.

Figure 6: Incoming Call, Device Locked

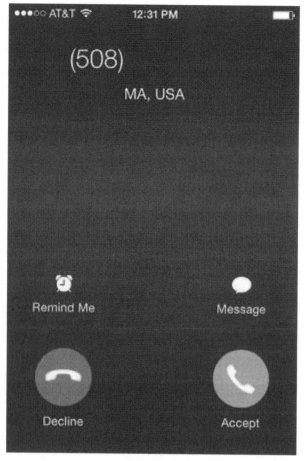

Figure 7: Incoming Call, Device Unlocked

6. Replying to an Incoming Call with a Text Message

During an incoming call, you may reject it and automatically send a text message to the caller. To reply to an incoming call with a text message.

1. Touch **Message** during an incoming voice call. A list of pre-defined text messages appear.
2. Touch a message. The selected text message is sent to the caller. Alternatively, touch **Custom** to enter your own text message.
3. Touch **Send**. The device sends the custom text message to the caller.

7. Setting a Reminder to Return an Incoming Call

During an incoming call, you may reject it and automatically set a reminder for yourself to return the call at a specified time or when you reach a specific location (such as work or home). To set a reminder to return an incoming call:

1. Touch **Remind Me** during an incoming voice call. The following reminder options appear: 'In 1 hour' and 'When I leave'.
2. Touch **In 1 hour**. The device displays a pop-up after one hour has passed reminding you to call back. Alternatively, touch **When I leave** to have the device remind you when you leave your current location.

8. Using the Speakerphone During a Voice Call

The device has a built-in Speakerphone, which is useful when calling from a car or when several people need to hear the conversation. To use the Speakerphone during a phone call:

1. Place a voice call. The Calling Screen appears, as shown in **Figure 8**.
2. Touch the icon. The Speakerphone is turned on. Adjust the volume of the Speakerphone by using the Volume Controls. Refer to **Button Layout** to locate the Volume Controls.
3. Touch the icon. The Speakerphone is turned off.

Figure 8: Calling Screen

9. Using the Keypad During a Voice Call

You may wish to use the keypad while on a call in order to input numbers in an automated menu or to enter an account number. To use the keypad during a phone call, place a voice call and touch the ▦ icon. The keypad appears. To hide the keypad again, touch **Hide**.

10. Using the Mute Function During a Voice Call

During a voice call, you may wish to mute your side of the conversation. When mute is turned on, the person on the other end of the line will not hear anything on your side. To use Mute during a call, place a voice call and touch the ![mute icon] icon. The device mutes your voice and the caller(s) can no longer hear you, but you are still able to hear them. Touch the ![mute icon] icon. Mute is turned off.

11. Putting a Caller on Hold (hidden button)

Apple replaced the Hold button (![pause icon]) with the ![button] button on the iPhone 4 and later generations. However, the Hold function still exists. Press and hold the ![mute button] button while on a call until the ![pause] button appears. Release the screen. The call is put on hold.

12. Starting a Conference Call (Adding a Call)

To talk to more than one person at a time, call another person while continuing the current call. To create a conference call, place a voice call and then touch the ![plus icon] icon. The list of contacts or the keypad is shown. Dial a number or select a contact to call. The first contact is put on hold while the device dials and connects to the second. Touch the ![merge icon] icon. A three-way conference call is created, as shown in **Figure 9**.

Note: Up to six lines may be included in a conference call.

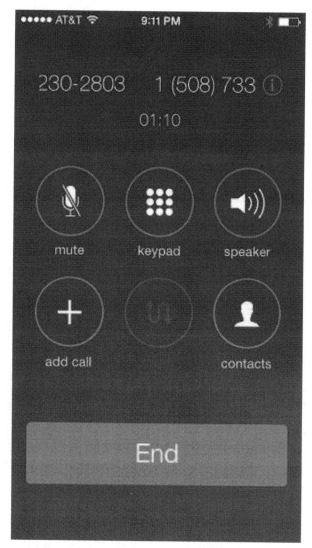

Figure 9: Three-Way Conference Call

13. Making a Call Over Wi-Fi

You can make calls using your Wi-Fi connection if you do not have any service, or to avoid using up your minutes. Calls over Wi-Fi connection will often be clearer and less prone to being dropped. To make a call using Wi-Fi, you must first turn on the feature. To turn on Wi-Fi Calling:

1. Touch the ⚙ icon. The Settings screen appears, as shown in **Figure 10**.
2. Scroll down and touch **Phone**. The Phone Settings screen appears, as shown in **Figure 11**.
3. Touch **Wi-Fi Calling**. The Wi-Fi Calling settings appear, as shown in **Figure 12**.
4. Touch the ⬭ switch next to **Wi-Fi Calling on This iPhone**. Wi-Fi Calling is turned on.

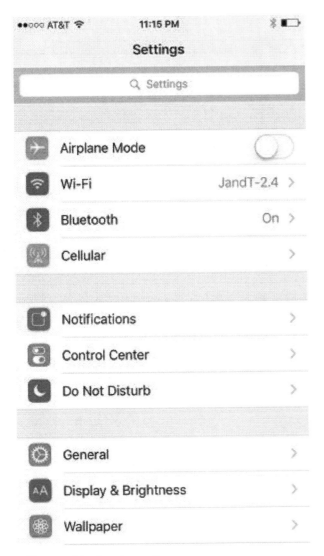

Figure 10: Settings Screen

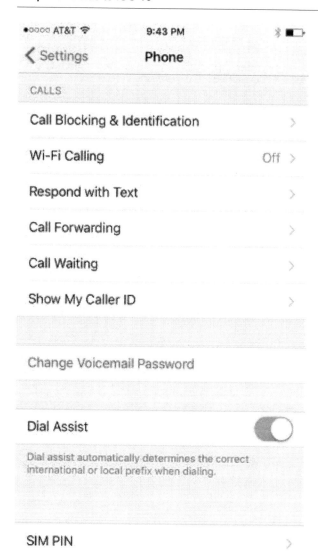

Figure 11: Phone Settings Screen

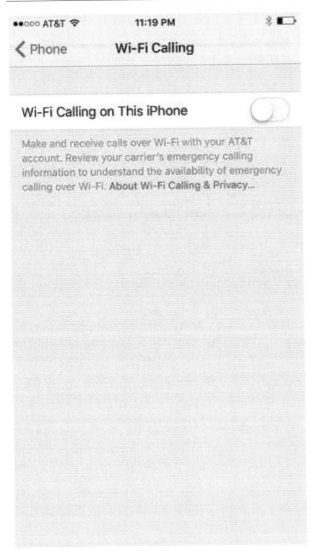

Figure 12: Wi-Fi Calling Settings

14. Starting a Facetime Call

iOS 10 devices have the ability to place video calls to other devices, such as iPads, Macs, or iPods (third generation and higher). Facetime does not require a Wi-Fi connection. You can place and receive FaceTime calls using a 4G connection (provided that you have at least one bar of service). However, using Wi-Fi may still provide a better video calling experience. You may also place a Facetime voice call if you do not wish to use the camera. Refer to *"Using Wi-Fi"* on page 40 to learn how to turn it on. To place a Facetime call:

1. Touch the [icon] icon on the Home screen. The Phonebook appears.
2. Touch the name of a contact. The Contact Information screen appears.

3. Touch the  icon to place a FaceTime call with video, or touch the 📞 icon to place a FaceTime call with only audio (iPad only). A Facetime call is placed. A high-pitched beeping sound plays until the call connects.

4. Touch the 🔄 button at any time to switch cameras, as outlined in **Figure 13**. Using this feature, you can either show your contact what you are seeing or show them your face.

iOS 10 devices can also receive FaceTime calls. To receive an incoming FaceTime call, touch **Accept**.

Note: You cannot place a FaceTime call to a device that is not compatible with FaceTime. The icon does not appear on the Contact Information screen, if the contact's device cannot use FaceTime.

Figure 13: Switch Camera Icon

Managing Contacts

Table of Contents

1. Adding a New Contact
2. Finding a Contact
3. Deleting a Contact
4. Editing Contact Information
5. Sharing a Contact's Information
6. Changing the Contact Sort Order

1. Adding a New Contact

iOS 10 devices can store phone numbers, email addresses, and other contact information in the phonebook. To add a new contact to the phonebook:

Note: For some unexplained reason, Apple has decided to place the Contacts icon in the Extras folder by default. If you cannot find it, look in that folder.

1. Touch the ▨ icon on the Home screen. The phonebook appears.
2. Touch the ✚ button at the top of the screen. The New Contact screen appears, as shown in **Figure 1**.
3. Touch **First**. The keyboard appears. Enter the first name of the contact.
4. Touch **Last**. Enter the last name of the contact.
5. Touch any empty field to enter the desired information, and then touch **Done** in the upper right-hand corner of the screen. The contact's information is stored.

Note: Refer to "Tips and Tricks" on page 293 to learn how to add an extension after the contact's phone number (iPhone only).

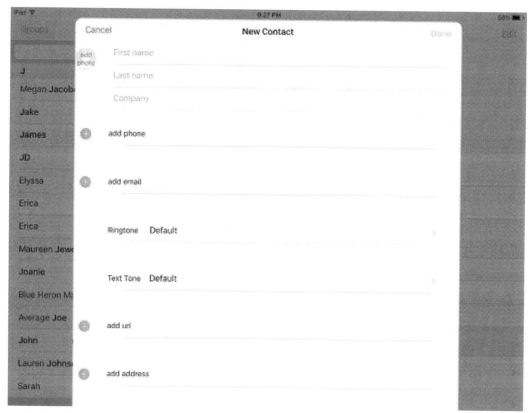

Figure 1: New Contact Screen

2. Finding a Contact

After adding contacts to your device's phonebook, you may search for them. To find a stored contact:

1. Touch the 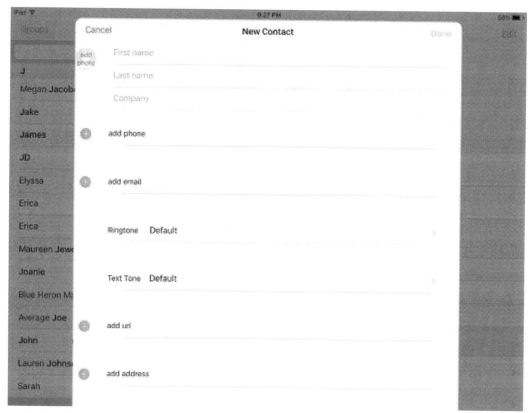 icon on the Home screen. The phonebook appears.
2. Touch **Search** at the top of the screen. The keyboard appears.
3. Start typing the name of a contact. Contact matches appear as you type, as shown in **Figure 2**.
4. Touch a match. The Contact Info screen appears, as shown in **Figure 3**.

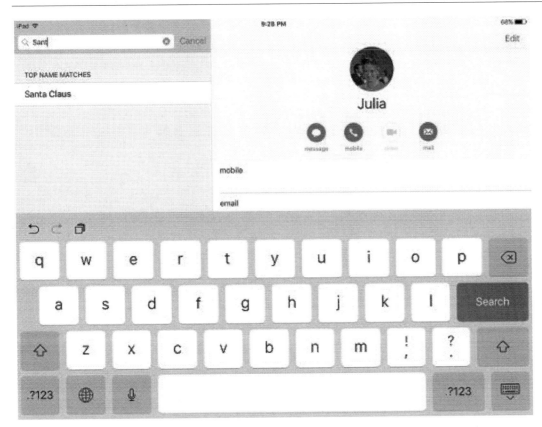

Figure 2: Contact Matches

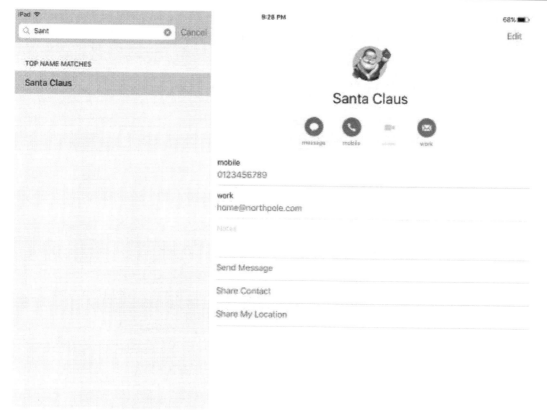

Figure 3: Contact Info Screen

3. Deleting a Contact

You may delete contact information from your phonebook in order to free up space, or for organizational purposes. To delete unwanted contact information:

Warning: There is no way to restore contact information after it has been deleted.

1. Touch the icon on the Home screen. The phonebook appears. If a list of all contacts does not appear, touch **All Contacts** in the upper left-hand corner of the screen to view the list.
2. Find and touch the name of the contact that you wish to delete. The Contact Info screen appears. Refer to **Finding a Contact** to learn how to search for a contact.
3. Touch **Edit** at the top of the screen. The Contact Information Editing screen appears.
4. Scroll down, and touch **Delete Contact** at the bottom of the screen, as shown in **Figure 4**. A Confirmation menu appears.

5. Touch **Delete Contact** again. The contact's information is deleted, and will no longer appear in your phonebook.

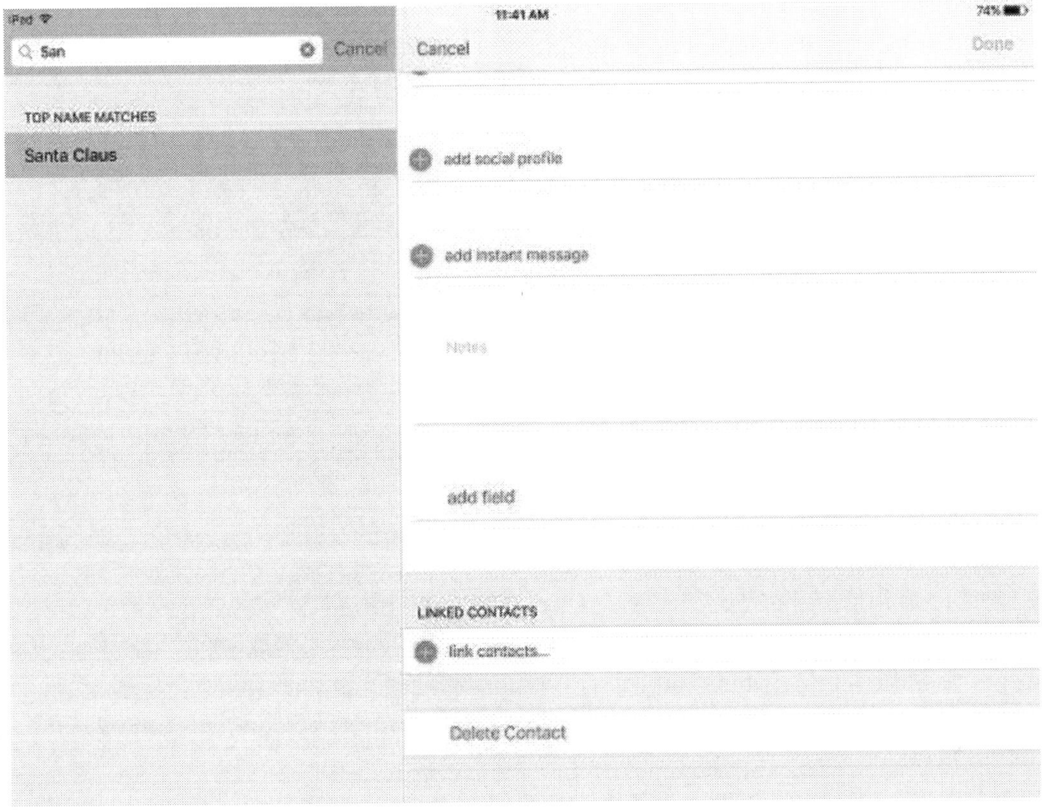

Figure 4: Delete Contact Screen

4. Editing Contact Information

After adding contacts to your phonebook, you may edit them at any time. To edit an existing contact's information:

1. Touch the ![icon] icon on the Home screen. The phonebook appears. If a list of all contacts does not appear, touch **All Contacts** in the upper left-hand corner of the screen to view the list.
2. Find and touch a contact's name. The Contact Info screen appears. Refer to *"Finding a Contact"* on page 70 to learn how to search for a contact.
3. Touch **Edit** at the top of the screen. The Contact Editing screen appears.
4. Touch a field to edit the corresponding information. Touch **Done** at the top of the screen when you are finished. The contact's information is updated.

5. Sharing a Contact's Information

You can share a contact's information, including their phone number, email and street addresses, and more. To share a contact's information with someone else:

1. Touch the ▦ icon. The phonebook appears. If a list of all contacts does not appear, touch **All Contacts** in the upper left-hand corner of the screen to view the list.
2. Find and touch a contact's name. The Contact Info screen appears. Refer to *"Finding a Contact"* on page 70 to learn how.
3. Touch **Share Contact** at the bottom of the contact's information. The Sharing Options menu appears at the bottom of the screen, as shown in **Figure 5**.
4. Follow the steps in the appropriate section below to email or text the contact's information:

To send the contact's information via email:

1. Touch the ✉ icon in the Sharing Options menu. The New Email screen appears, as shown in **Figure 6**. Choose one of the following options for entering the email address:
   - Start typing the name of the contact with whom you wish to share the information. The matching contacts appear. Touch the contact's name. The contact's email address is added.
   - Enter the email address from scratch. To use a number, touch the **123** button at the bottom left of the screen. When done, touch the **return** button in the lower right-hand corner of the screen. Enter more addresses if needed.
   - Touch the ⊕ icon to select contacts from your phonebook, or enter as many email addresses as you wish.
2. Enter an optional subject by touching **Subject**, and touch **CC** to add other addresses to which to send the information.
3. Touch **Send** at the top of the screen. The contact's information is sent to the selected email addresses.

To send a contact's information via multimedia message, touch the ⬤ icon in the Sharing Options menu. The New Message screen appears, as shown in **Figure 7**. Enter the phone number or phone numbers, and touch **Send**. The contact's information is sent. There are three methods for entering the phone number:

- Start typing the name of the contact with whom you wish to share the information. Matching contacts appear. Touch the contact's name. The contact's number is added.
- Type the phone number from scratch. To use numbers, touch the **123** button at the bottom left of the screen. When done, touch the ▉return▉ button in the lower right-hand corner of the screen.
- Touch the ⊕ icon to select one or more contacts from the phonebook.

Figure 5: Sharing Options Menu

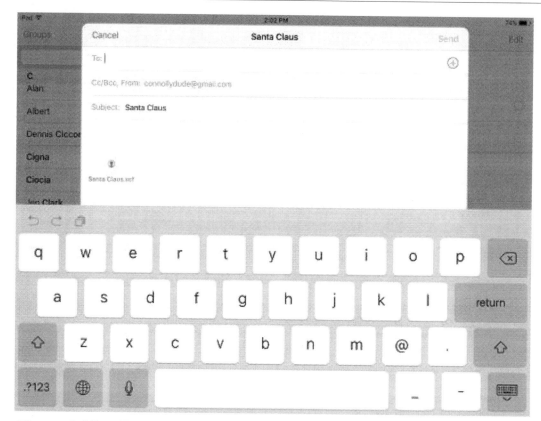

Figure 6: New Email Screen

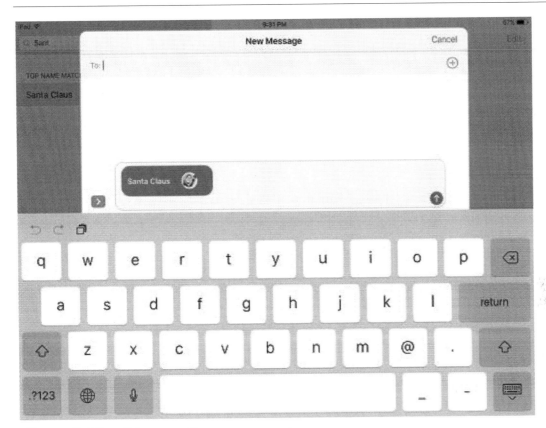

Figure 7: New Message Screen

6. Changing the Contact Sort Order

By default, the device sorts the contacts in the phonebook by last name. For instance, if the names Jane Doe and John Johnson are in the phonebook, John Johnson would come after Jane Doe because 'J' comes after 'D' in the English alphabet. To change the sort order:

1. Touch the icon. The Settings screen appears, as shown in **Figure 8**.
2. Scroll down, and touch **Contacts**. The Contacts Settings screen appears, as shown in **Figure 9**.
3. Touch **Sort Order**. The Sort Order screen appears, as shown in **Figure 10**.
4. Touch **First, Last**. A check mark appears to the right of the option, and the contacts will be sorted by first name.
5. Touch **Last, First**. A check mark appears to the right of the option, and the contacts will be sorted by last name.

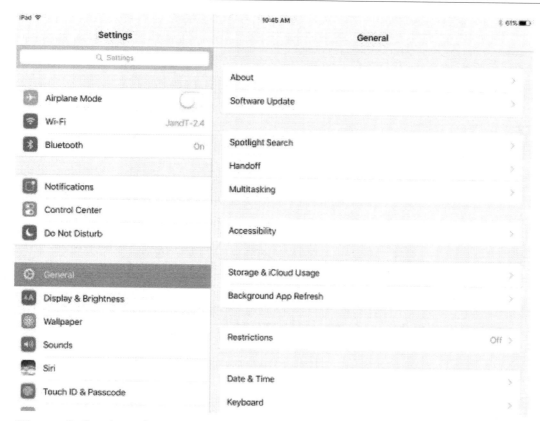

Figure 8: Settings Screen

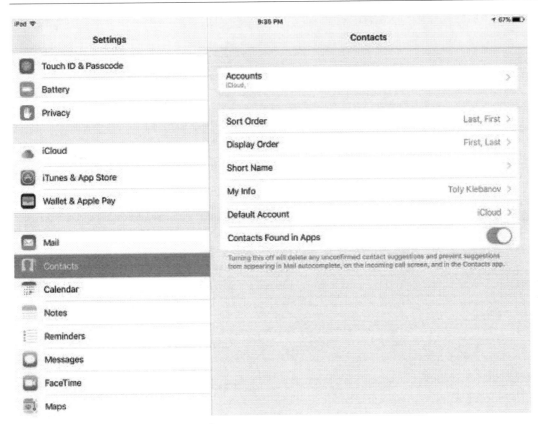

Figure 9: Contacts Settings Screen

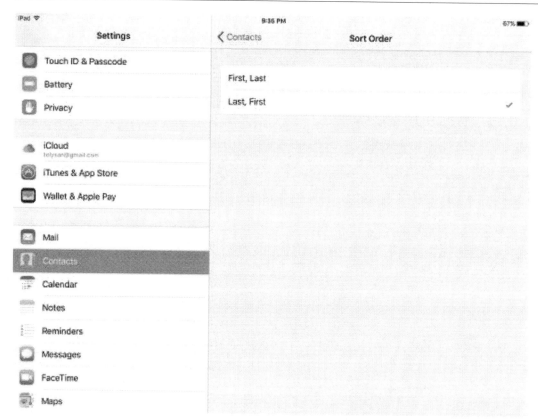

Figure 10: Sort Order Screen

Text Messaging

Table of Contents

1. Composing a New Text Message
2. Copying, Cutting, and Pasting Text
3. Using the Spell Check Feature
4. Receiving a Text Message
5. Reading a Stored Text Message
6. Forwarding a Text Message
7. Calling the Sender from within a Text (iPhone Only)
8. Viewing Sender Information from within a Text
9. Deleting a Text Message
10. Adding Texted Phone Numbers to the Phonebook
11. Sending a Picture Message
12. Leaving a Group Conversation
13. Naming a Conversation
14. Adding a Voice Message to a Conversation (iMessage Only)
15. Sharing Your Location in a Conversation
16. Viewing All Attachments in a Conversation
17. Handwriting a Message
18. Sending a Digital Touch
19. Using Tapback in a Message
20. Turning Read Receipts for a Single Conversation On or Off
21. Using iMessage Applications

1. Composing a New Text Message

iOS 10 devices can send text messages to other mobile phones, tablets, and Macs. To compose a new message:

1. Touch the icon on the Home screen. The Messages screen appears, as shown in **Figure 1**.

2. Touch the icon. The New Message screen appears, as shown in **Figure 2**.

3. Enter the phone number of the recipient. There are three options for entering this information:

- Start typing the name of the contact. Matching contacts appear as you type. Touch the contact's name. The contact's number is added.
- Enter the phone number from scratch.
- Touch the ⊕ button to select a contact from the Phonebook. Add as many numbers as desired.

4. Touch the text field. The cursor starts flashing at the beginning of the field.

5. Enter your message. If you begin to type a word incorrectly, the device may give you a suggestion. Touch the suggestion to use it.

6. Touch the ↑ button or the ↑ button when finished. The button that appears depends on whether the recipient is using iMessage, in which case the text message is free to send. The message is sent. Your most recent message is shown in a gray bubble on the left side of the screen, as shown in **Figure 3** (the image may vary slightly on the iPad). All text messages are shown in conversation view.

To send a new message to someone you have already texted:

1. Touch the ⬜ icon on the Home screen. The Messages screen appears.
2. Touch the name or number of the recipient. The Conversation screen appears. If the name is not in the list, try scrolling down by touching the screen and moving your finger up. If you cannot find the name, you may have deleted your conversation with that contact.
3. Touch the text field. The cursor starts flashing, and a keyboard is shown.

4. Enter the message and then touch the ↑ button or the ↑ button when finished. The message is sent. Touch the screen and move your finger down to scroll through older messages.

Figure 1: Messages Screen

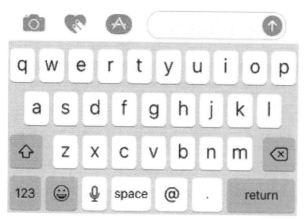

Figure 2: New Message Screen

Figure 3: Your Message in a Gray Bubble

2. Copying, Cutting, and Pasting Text

The device allows you to copy or cut text from one location and paste it to another. Copying leaves the text in its current location and allows you to paste it elsewhere. Cutting deletes the text from its current location and allows you to paste it elsewhere. To cut, copy, and paste text:

1. Touch and hold text in a text field or in a conversation. The Select menu appears above the text, as shown in **Figure 4**. Refer to *"Composing a New Text Message"* on page 81 to learn how to compose a text.
2. Touch **Select All**. All of the text is selected. To select a single word, touch **Select**. Blue dots appear around the word or phrase.
3. Touch and hold one of the blue dots and drag it in any direction. The text between the dots is highlighted and a text menu appears, as shown in **Figure 5**.
4. Touch **Cut** or **Copy**. The corresponding action is taken, and the text is ready to be pasted.
5. Touch and hold any empty text field, and then touch **Paste**. The text is inserted.

Note: Refer to "Tips and Tricks" *on page 293 to learn more about editing text.*

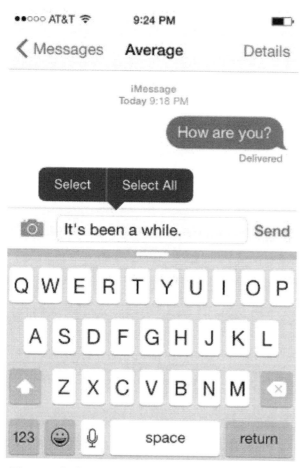

Figure 4: Select Menu

Figure 5: Text Menu

3. Using the Spell Check Feature

The device will make suggestions for words that are spelled incorrectly. Touch a suggestion to substitute the word immediately. If auto-correction is enabled, the device will automatically replace common typos. Over time, the device will learn your most commonly typed words, even names and slang. Refer to *"Adjusting Language and Keyboard Settings"* on page 235 to learn more about auto-correction.

4. Receiving a Text Message

The device can receive text messages from any other mobile device. When the device receives a text, it vibrates once (iPhone only) or plays a sound, depending on the settings. The New Message notification appears on the Lock screen, as shown in **Figure 6**, or on the Home screen, as shown in **Figure 7**. Whether the notification appears in the Notification Bar or on the Home screen depends on your settings. Use the following tips when receiving text messages:

- Slide the text notification to the right on the Lock screen to open the text message.
- Touch the text message alert on the Home screen or while using an application to open the text message. Slide down on the alert to reply quickly. The Quick Reply window appears, as shown in **Figure 8**. Slide down again to close the Quick Reply window. To reply without opening the Messages application, enter a reply and touch **Send**.

- The icon next to the icon on the Home screen indicates that there is one unread message. This number changes depending on the number of unread messages. The number in the red circle will not disappear until the message is read. Touch the icon to view the message.

Note: Refer to "Composing a New Text Message" *on page 81 to learn more about sending text messages.*

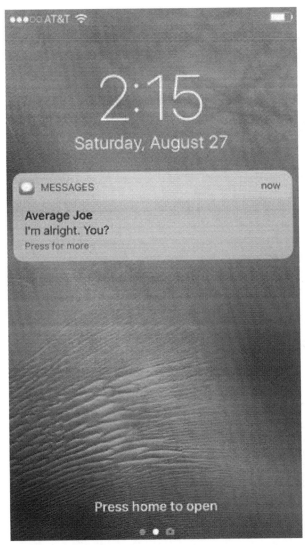

Figure 6: New Message Notification on the Lock Screen

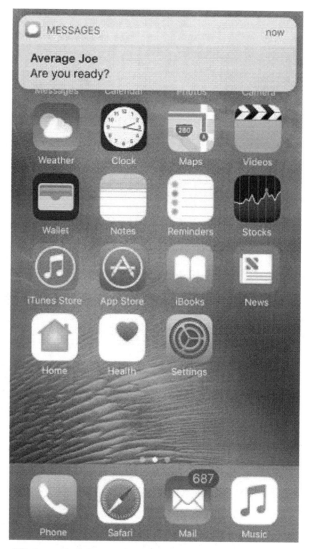

Figure 7: New Message Notification on the Home Screen

Figure 8: Quick Message Reply Window

5. Reading a Stored Text Message

You may read any text messages that you have received, provided that you have not deleted them. To read stored text messages:

1. Touch the ⬜ icon on the Home screen. The Messages screen appears. The device organizes conversations based on the date the last message in the conversation was sent or received, with the most recent conversation at the top of the list.
2. Touch the name of a contact to view the conversation. The Conversation screen appears.
3. Touch the screen, and move your finger up or down to scroll through the conversation. The most recent messages appear at the bottom.

6. Forwarding a Text Message

Forwarding a message copies the contents of the original message when you wish to send it to a new recipient. You may wish to forward a text message to save yourself some time entering the same message. To forward a text message:

1. Touch the ⬜ icon on the Home screen. The Messages screen appears, displaying each sender's name on the left and the date of the message on the right.
2. Touch the conversation that contains the message(s) that you wish to forward. The Conversation screen appears.
3. Touch and hold a message in the conversation. The Message menu appears above the message, as shown in **Figure 9**.
4. Touch **More**. A blue check mark appears next to the message, as shown in **Figure 10**.
5. Touch the ⤳ button at the bottom of the screen. The New Message screen appears, with the selected message copied into the text field.
6. Start typing the name of a contact or touch the ⊕ icon to select a number from the Phonebook. The contact is added to the Addressee list.
7. Touch the ⬆ button or the ⬆ button. The message is forwarded to the contacts in the 'To:' field.

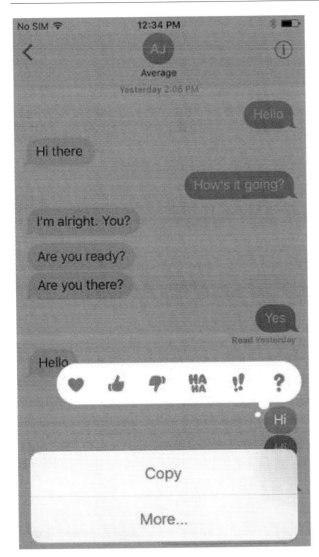

Figure 9: Message Menu

Figure 10: Selected Messages

7. Calling the Sender from within a Text (iPhone Only)

After receiving a text message from a contact, you may call that person without ever exiting the text message. To call someone from whom you have received a text message:

1. Touch the ⬜ icon on the Home screen. The Messages screen appears. The device organizes conversations based on the date the last message in the conversation was sent or received, with the most recent conversation at the top of the list.
2. Touch the conversation that contains the message(s) from the sender that you wish to call. The Conversation screen appears.

3. Touch the ⓘ button at the top of the screen. The Conversation Details screen appears, as shown in **Figure 11**.

4. Touch the 📞 icon. The iPhone places the call.

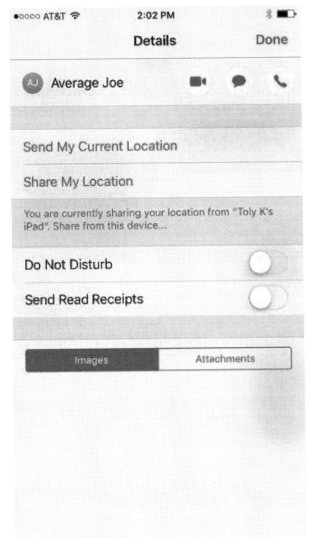

Figure 11: Conversation Details Screen

8. Viewing Sender Information from within a Text

If you have stored a contact's information in the Phonebook, you may view it at any time without leaving a text conversation between the two of you. To view the information of a contact who sent you a message:

1. Touch the icon on the Home screen. The Messages screen appears.
2. Touch a conversation. The Conversation screen appears.
3. Touch the screen and move your finger down until the top of the conversation appears.
4. Touch the contact's name at the top of the screen. The Contact Information screen appears.

9. Deleting a Text Message

The device can delete separate text messages or an entire conversation, which is a series of text messages between you and a contact.

Warning: Once deleted, text messages cannot be restored.

To delete an entire conversation:

1. Touch the icon on the Home screen. The Messages screen appears.
2. Touch and hold a message in a conversation, and slide your finger to the left. 'Delete' appears.
3. Touch **Delete**. The entire conversation is deleted.

To delete a separate text message:

1. Touch the icon on the Home screen. The Messages screen appears.
2. Touch a conversation. The conversation opens.
3. Touch and hold a message in a conversation. The message menu appears.
4. Touch **More**. Touch any other messages that you wish to delete. A mark appears next to each selected message.
5. Touch the icon at the bottom of the screen. A confirmation dialog appears.
6. Touch **Delete Message**. The selected messages are deleted.

10. Adding Texted Phone Numbers to the Phonebook

A phone number sent via text message can be added to your Phonebook immediately. To add a texted phone number to your Phonebook:

1. Touch the ⬤ icon on the Home screen. The Messages screen appears.
2. Touch a conversation. The Conversation screen appears.
3. Touch and hold the phone number in the conversation. The Phone Number menu appears, as shown in **Figure 12**. On an iPad, the Phone Number menu appears above the phone number.
4. Touch **Add to Contacts**. The Info screen appears.
5. Touch **Create New Contact** or **Add to Existing Contact**. The New Contact screen appears, with the phone number field filled in, as shown in **Figure 13**. If you touched 'Add to Existing Contact', the Phonebook appears, and you may choose the contact that you want to modify.
6. Enter the contact's information, then touch **Done.** The contact is added to your Phonebook.

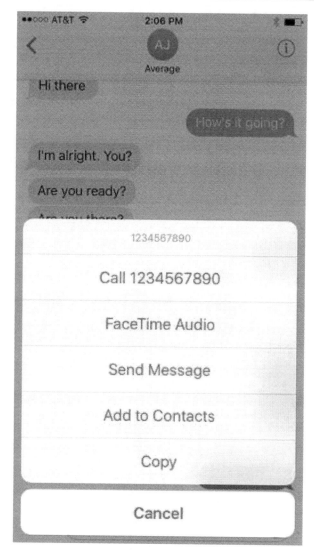

Figure 12: Phone Number Menu

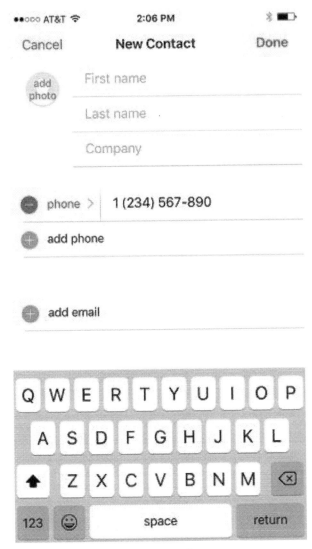

Figure 13: New Contact Screen

11. Sending a Picture Message

You may attach a picture to any text message that you send.

To send a picture message:

1. Touch the ⬜ icon on the Home screen. The Messages screen appears.

2. Touch the ✎ icon. The New Message screen appears.

3. Touch the 📷 button to the left of the text field. The Photo Attachment menu appears and the camera turns on, as shown in **Figure 14**. If you do not see the 📷 button touch the ▶ button first.

4. Follow the steps in one of the sections below to either attach an existing picture or take a picture to send:

To attach an existing picture to the text message:

1. Touch **Photo Library**. A list of Photo Albums appears, as shown in **Figure 15**.
2. Touch a photo album. The photo album opens.
3. Touch a photo. The preview of the photo appears.
4. Touch **Choose**. The photo is attached to the text message. Alternatively, touch **Cancel** to select a different photo.
5. Touch the ⬆ button or the ⬆ button. The picture message is sent.

To take a picture and attach it to the text message:

1. Touch **Take Photo or Video**. The camera turns on, as shown in **Figure 16**. You can also capture a photo immediately by touching the ⬜ button in the Photo Attachment menu.

2. Touch the ⬜ button at the bottom of the screen. The photo is captured and a preview of the photo appears.

3. Touch **Done** to use the photo in the message, or touch **Retake** to discard the picture and take another one. The photo is attached. Alternatively, touch **Cancel** while the camera is turned on to return to the conversation without taking a picture.

4. Touch the ⬆ button or the ⬆ button. The picture message is sent.

Note: Up to nine photos may be sent in a picture message.

Figure 14: Photo Attachment Menu

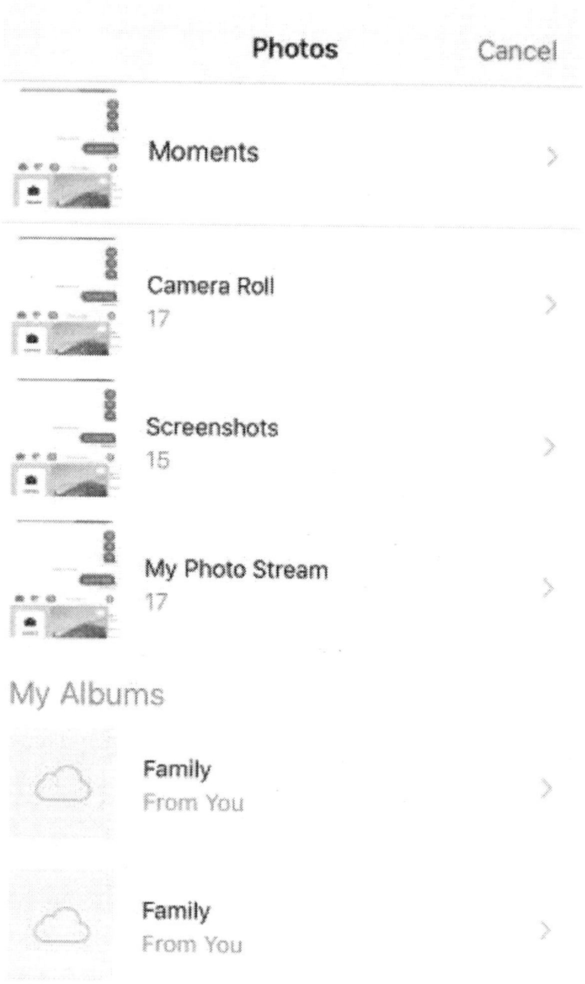

Figure 15: List of Photo Albums

Figure 16: Camera Turned On

12. Leaving a Group Conversation

You may remove yourself from a group conversation if you no longer wish to participate. Once removed, you will not receive any further messages in that conversation. To leave a group conversation:

1. Touch **Details** at the top of the conversation. The Conversation details appear.
2. Touch **Leave this Conversation**. A confirmation dialog appears.
3. Touch **Leave this Conversation** again. You are removed from the conversation.

Note: This feature may not be available on the iPad.

13. Naming a Conversation

In order to find it more quickly and easily, you may name a conversation with a group. The title of the conversation will show up on the device of everyone involved in the conversation. To name a conversation:

1. Touch **Details** at the top of the conversation. The Conversation details appear.
2. Touch the ⓘ button at the top of the screen. The Conversation Details screen appears.
3. Touch **Enter a Group Name**, then enter the title of the conversation. The conversation is renamed.

14. Adding a Voice Message to a Conversation (iMessage Only)

You may add a short voice message to a text message or conversation. This feature only works when using iMessage. If you send a text message to someone who does not use an iPhone, or has not registered for iMessage, this feature will not work. To add a voice message to an iMessage:

1. Touch and hold the 🎤 button to the right of the text field. The microphone turns on.
2. Speak the voice message that you would like to attach. When you are finished, release the 🎤 button. The voice message is recorded, as shown in **Figure 17**.
3. Touch the ⬆ button. The voice message is sent. You can also slide your finger up to the ⬆ button without letting go of the screen to immediately send the voice message. Alternatively, let go of the screen, then touch the ▶ icon to preview the voice message. Touch the ✕ icon if you would like to discard the voice message.

Figure 17: Recorded Voice Message

15. Sharing Your Location in a Conversation

You may choose to share your location with a contact or a number of participants in a conversation. To share your location for a specified amount of time:

1. Touch the ⓘ button at the top of the screen. The Conversation Details screen appears.
2. Touch **Share My Location**. The Location Sharing menu appears, as shown in **Figure 18**.

3. Touch one of the following options to share your location for the corresponding amount of time: **Share for One Hour**, **Share Until End of Day**, or **Share Indefinitely**. You location is shared. The last option will allow you to share your location until you touch **Stop Sharing My Location** on the Conversation Details screen.

You can also touch **Send My Current Location** to share your location once immediately.

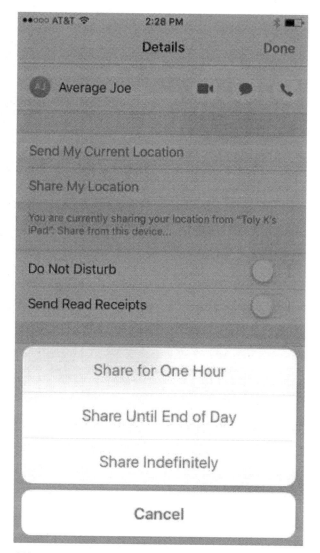

Figure 18: Location Sharing Menu

16. Viewing All Attachments in a Conversation

The Messaging application provides a convenient way to view all of the pictures, videos, and voice messages attached to a conversation in one neat list. To view all attachments in a conversation, touch the (i) button at the top of a conversation. The Conversation details appear and the list of attachments is shown at the bottom of the screen. To save one of the attachments in the list to a photo album:

1. Touch the attachment that you want to save. The attachment appears in full screen.
2. Touch the center of the screen. The Attachment menu appears, as shown in **Figure 19**.

3. Touch the ⬆ icon at the top of the screen, if it is a photo, or at the bottom of the screen, if it is a video. The Save Photo menu appears, as shown in **Figure 20**, or the Save Video menu appears, as shown in **Figure 21**.

4. Touch the ⬇ icon. The attachment is saved to the Recently Added album on your device.

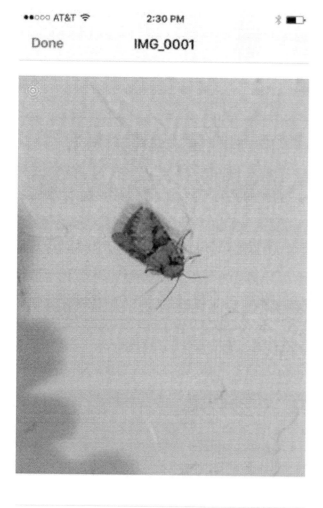

Figure 19: Attachment Menu

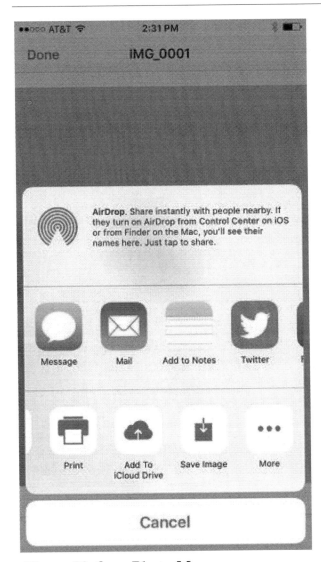

Figure 20: Save Photo Menu

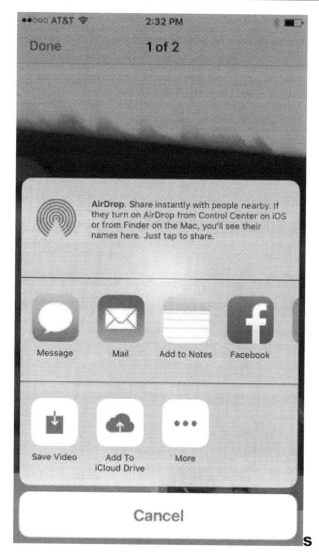

Figure 21: Save Video Menu

17. Handwriting a Message

You can send a handwritten message when using iMessage, which plays animated handwriting on the recipient's screen. To send a handwritten message:

1. While viewing a text conversation, rotate the phone to view it in Landscape mode. The Handwriting screen appears, as shown in **Figure 22**.
2. Write the message using your finger. Do NOT use a pen or stylus. If you do not have enough space touch the right-facing arrow to move to the next are of the Handwriting screen.

3. Touch **Done**. The Conversation screen appears with the message entered.

4. Touch the 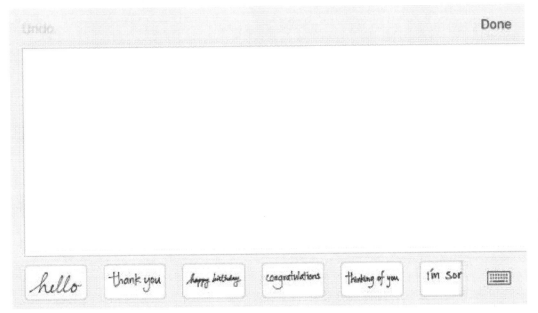 button. The handwritten message is sent.

Figure 22: Handwriting Screen

---

18. Sending a Digital Touch

You can send a heartbeat or tap sequence in a message. This types of message is called Digital Touch. To send a Digital Touch, touch the icon and then tap the screen in the preferred manner. Play around with it. You can touch on of the hand icons on the right side of the screen for more tips.

---

19. Using Tapback in a Message

When you receive a message in iMessage, you can immediately respond with an emoji that appears directly on the person's original message. For example, you can send a thumbs up or a heart that appears on the original message. This feature is compatible with text and multimedia messages, such as pictures, videos, or Digital Touches. To send a Tapback, touch and hold the text message in the conversation. The Message menu appears. Touch a Tapback, such as a heart or thumbs up. The Tapback is sent immediately.

20. Turning Read Receipts for a Single Conversation On or Off

After receiving and opening a message from an iPhone, iPad, or iPod Touch, your device can notify the sender that you have opened and read the message. These notifications are called Read Receipts, and appear under the original message on the sender's screen as "Read", followed by a time. Prior to iOS 10, you could turn read receipts off for the iMessage application. It is now possible to turn on or off Read Receipts for a single conversation. To turn Read Receipts on or off for a conversation:

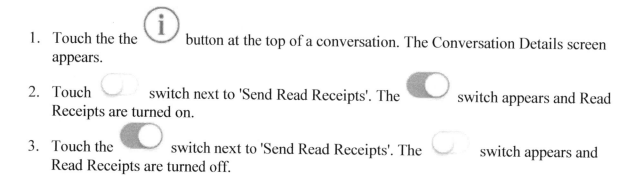

1. Touch the the ⓘ button at the top of a conversation. The Conversation Details screen appears.

2. Touch ⬭ switch next to 'Send Read Receipts'. The ⬬ switch appears and Read Receipts are turned on.

3. Touch the ⬬ switch next to 'Send Read Receipts'. The ⬭ switch appears and Read Receipts are turned off.

21. Using iMessage Applications

There are certain applications that can now interact with iMessage. Each iMessage application in the App Store is indicated by the label "Offers iMessage App'. Download the application and access it from iMessage by touching the 🅰 button. Then, touch the ⦿⦿ button. The list of installed iMessage applications appears, as shown in **Figure 23**. If you do not have any applications installed, touch **Store** to browse the available iMessage applications.

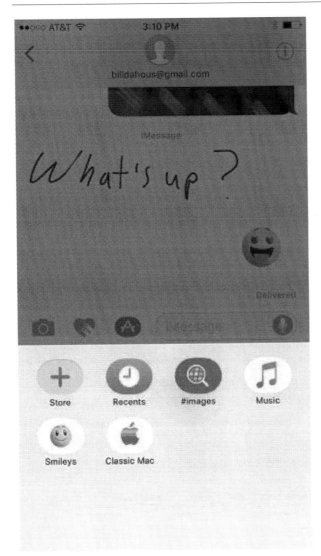

Figure 23: List of Installed iMessage Applications

Using the Safari Web Browser

Table of Contents

1. Navigating to a Website
2. Adding and Viewing Bookmarks
3. Adding a Bookmark to the Home Screen
4. Managing Open Browser Tabs
5. Blocking Pop-Up Windows
6. Changing the Search Engine
7. Clearing History and Browsing Data
8. Viewing an Article in Reader Mode
9. Turning Private Browsing On or Off
10. Setting Up the AutoFill Feature
11. Customizing the Smart Search Field
12. Viewing Recently Closed Tabs
13. Scanning a Credit Card Using the Device's Camera

1. Navigating to a Website

You can surf the web using your device. To navigate to a website using the web address:

1. Touch the ![Safari icon] icon on the Home screen. The Safari Web browser opens.
2. Touch the Address bar at the top of the screen, as outlined in **Figure 1**. The keyboard appears. If you do not see the Address bar, touch the screen and move your finger down to scroll up.
3. Touch the web address at the top of the screen. The address field is erased.
4. Enter a web address and touch **Go**. Safari navigates to the website.
5. Touch the ⟨ button. Safari navigates to the previous web page.
6. Touch the ⟩ button. Safari navigates to the next web page.

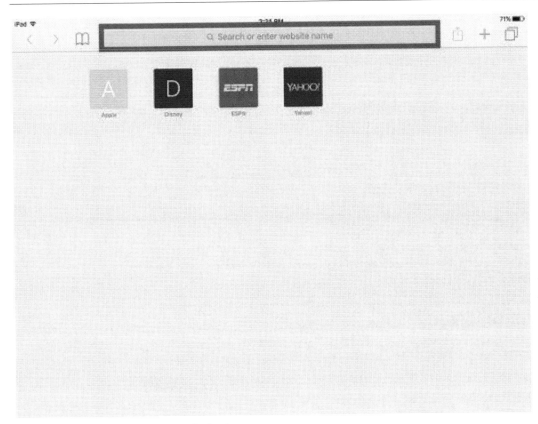

Figure 1: Address Bar in Safari

2. Adding and Viewing Bookmarks

The device can store favorite websites as Bookmarks to allow you to access them faster in the future. To add a Bookmark in Safari:

1. Touch the ![compass] icon on the Home screen. The Safari browser opens.
2. Navigate to a website. Refer to *"Navigating to a Website"* on page 114 to learn how.
3. Touch the ![share] button. The Bookmark menu appears, as shown in **Figure 2**.
4. Touch the ![book] icon. The Add Bookmark window appears, as shown in **Figure 3**.
5. Enter a name for the bookmark and touch **Save**. The website is added to the Bookmarks.
6. To view saved Bookmarks, touch the ![book] icon in the Safari browser. The Bookmarks screen appears, as shown in **Figure 4**. Touch a bookmark. Safari navigates to the indicated website.

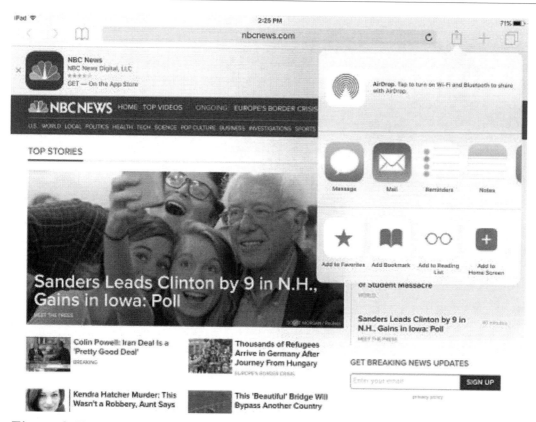

Figure 2: Bookmark Menu

Figure 3: Add Bookmark Window

Figure 4: Bookmarks Screen

3. Adding a Bookmark to the Home Screen

On the device, bookmarks can be added to the Home screen; they will then appear like application icons. To add a bookmark to the Home screen as an icon:

1. Touch the ![compass] icon on the Home screen. The Safari browser opens.
2. Navigate to a website. Refer to *"Navigating to a Website"* on page 114 to learn how.

3. Touch the ![share] button. The Bookmark menu appears.

4. Touch the ![plus] icon. The Add to Home window appears, as shown in **Figure 5**.
5. Enter a name for the bookmark and touch **Add**. The bookmark is added to the Home screen.

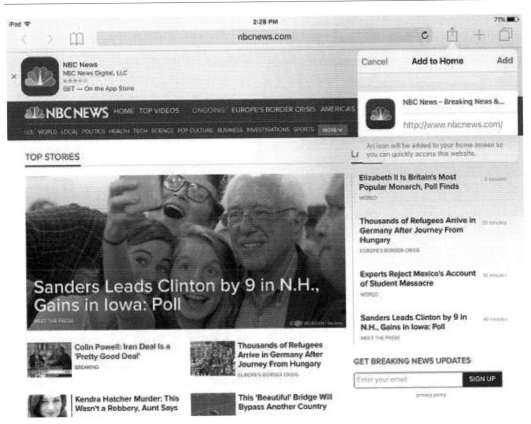

Figure 5: Add to Home Window

4. Managing Open Browser Tabs

The Safari Web browser supports an unlimited number of browser tabs. This feature is analogous to tabbed browsing in an internet browser like Firefox, Chrome, or Internet Explorer. Use the following tips when working with browser tabs:

- To view the open Safari tabs, touch the button in Safari. The open Safari tabs appear, as shown in **Figure 6**. Touch the screen and flick your finger up or down to view other open tabs. While viewing the open Safari tabs:

- To open a new browser tab, touch the button.
- To close a tab on the iPhone, touch the X in the upper left corner of the tab. On the iPad, touch the X on a tab to close it. You can also touch **Done** to return to the tab that you were just viewing.
- To reorder the tabs, touch and hold a tab, and move it up or down.

- To close all tabs at once, touch and hold the ⬜ button, and then touch **Close # Tabs**, where the # symbol represents the number of tabs that are currently open.

- To view two tabs at the same time in Split-Screen mode, touch and hold the ⬜ button, and then touch **Open Split View**. The screen is split and your currently open tabs appear on the left. A new tab opens on the right. You can open new tabs in the window on the right just as you would in a regular Safari session. To merge all tabs again, touch and hold the hold the ⬜ button, and then touch **Merge All Tabs**. You can also touch **Close Tab** to return to Full-Screen mode if you have only opened one tab in the window on the right.

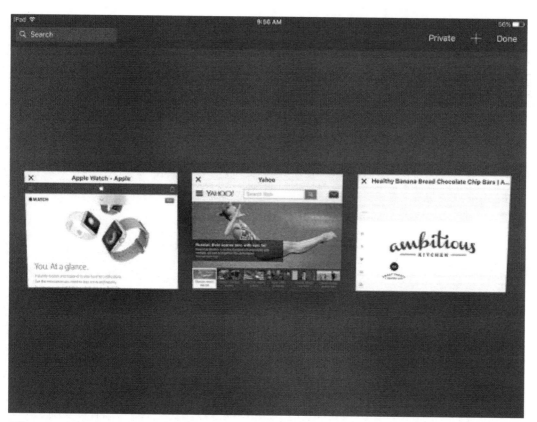

Figure 6: Open Safari Tabs

5. Blocking Pop-Up Windows

Some websites may have pop-up windows that interfere with browsing the internet. By default, pop-ups are already blocked. To block pop-ups:

1. Touch the ![icon] icon on the Home screen. The Settings screen appears, as shown in **Figure 7**.
2. Scroll down and touch **Safari**. The Safari Settings screen appears, as shown in **Figure 8**.
3. Touch the ⬭ switch next to 'Block Pop-Ups'. Pop-ups will now be blocked.
4. Touch the ⬤ switch next to 'Block Pop-Ups'. Pop-ups will now be allowed.

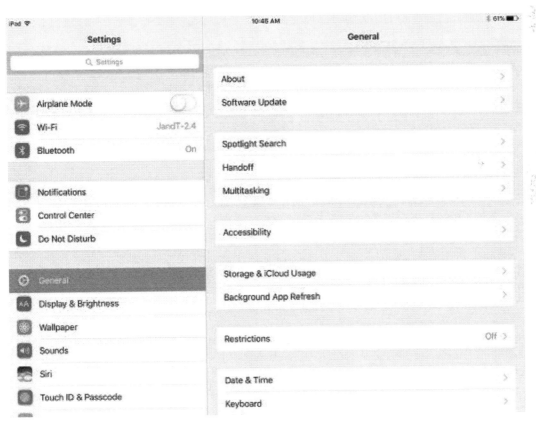

Figure 7: Settings Screen

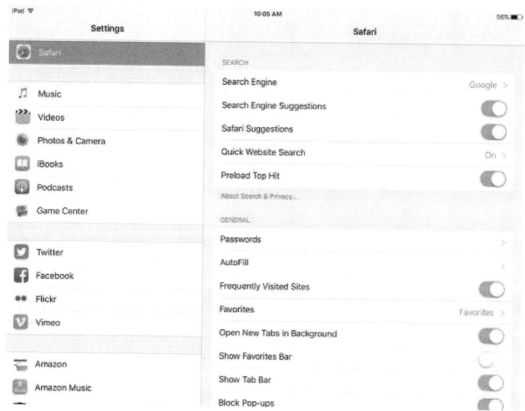

Figure 8: Safari Settings Screen

6. Changing the Search Engine

Google, Yahoo, or Bing can be set as the default search engine in Safari. When you get your new device, the default search engine is set to Google. The Address bar at the top of the screen also acts as a search field in Safari. To change the default search engine:

1. Touch the ⚙ icon on the Home screen. The Settings screen appears.
2. Touch **Safari**. The Safari Settings screen appears.
3. Touch **Search Engine**. A list of search engines appears.
4. Touch the preferred search engine. The default search engine is set, and its name will now appear in the empty search field.

7. Clearing the History and Browsing Data

The device can clear the list of recently visited websites, known as the History, as well as other data, such as saved passwords, known as Cookies. The device can also delete data from previously visited websites, known as the Cache. To delete all of these items:

1. Touch the icon on the Home screen. The Settings screen appears.
2. Touch **Safari**. The Safari Settings screen appears.
3. Touch **Clear History and Website Data**. A confirmation dialog appears.
4. Touch **Clear History and Data** (or touch **Clear**, if using an iPad). The selected data is deleted and the option is grayed out on the Safari Settings screen.

8. Viewing an Article in Reader Mode

The Safari browser can display certain news articles in Reader Mode, which allows you to read them like a book with no images or links. To view an article in Reader Mode, touch the button in the address bar (when available), as outlined in **Figure 9**. Reader Mode turns on, as shown in **Figure 10**. While in Reader Mode, you can customize the font by touching the ₳A When Reader Mode is available, "Reader View Available" briefly appears in the address bar when the page has finished loading.

Figure 9: Reader Button in the Address Bar

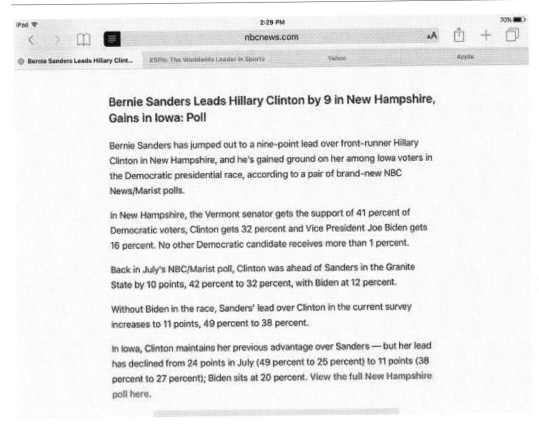

Figure 10: Article in Reader Mode

9. Turning Private Browsing On or Off

In order to preserve privacy, the Safari Web browser allows you to surf the internet without saving the History or any other data showing that you have visited a particular website. To open a private tab:

1. Touch the ⬜ button. The open browser tabs appear.
2. Touch **Private**. Private Mode is turned on.
3. Touch the ➕ icon to open a new private tab.
4. When you are ready to exit private mode, touch the ⬜ button, and then touch **Private** again.

10. Setting Up the AutoFill Feature

Safari can automatically fill in personal information, such as passwords and credit card information, to save you time when filling forms or shopping online. To set up the AutoFill feature:

1. Touch the ⚙ icon on the Home screen. The Settings screen appears.
2. Touch **Safari**. The Safari Settings screen appears.
3. Touch **AutoFill**. The Autofill screen appears, as shown in **Figure 11**.
4. Touch one of the following ⬭ switches turn on the corresponding AutoFill:

   - **Use Contact Info** - Enables the use of contact information when filling in forms. The Phonebook appears. Touch the name of a contact to use the contact information to fill in forms. It is recommended that you create a contact entry for yourself and use it for this feature.
   - **Names and Passwords** - Enables the use of saved names and passwords. You will be given the option to set up a security lock in order to keep your private information safe. Websites will give you the option to save your username and password. You can also touch the ⬭ switch next to 'Always Allow' to save passwords even for websites that will never save your password otherwise.
   - **Credit Cards** - Enables the use of saved credit card information. You will be given the option to set up a security lock in order to keep your private information safe. Touch **Saved Credit Cards**, and then touch **Add Credit Card** to add a new credit card.

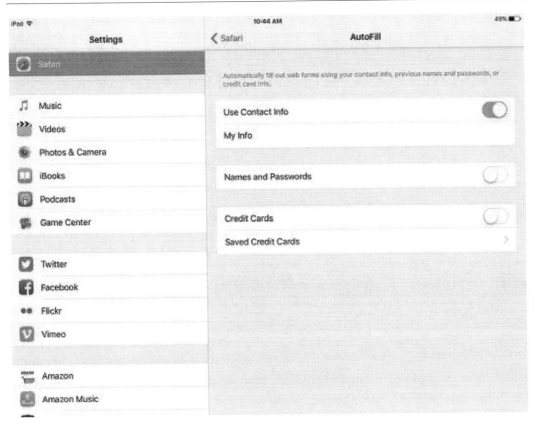

Figure 11: Autofill Screen

11. Customizing the Smart Search Field

The address bar in the Safari browser can act as a search field that assists you by matching your search terms while you type. To customize the smart search field:

1. Touch the ![icon] icon on the Home screen. The Settings screen appears.
2. Touch **Safari**. The Safari Settings screen appears.
3. Touch one of the following ![switch] switches to turn on the corresponding smart search feature:
   - **Search Engine Suggestions** - Enables search term matching to assist you when performing a search.
   - **Preload Top Hit** - Automatically loads the most popular search result when you perform a search. The web page is loaded in the background before you even touch the link.

12. Viewing Recently Closed Tabs

The Safari browser saves a history of all browser tabs that were recently closed. To view all recently closed browser tabs:

1. Touch the 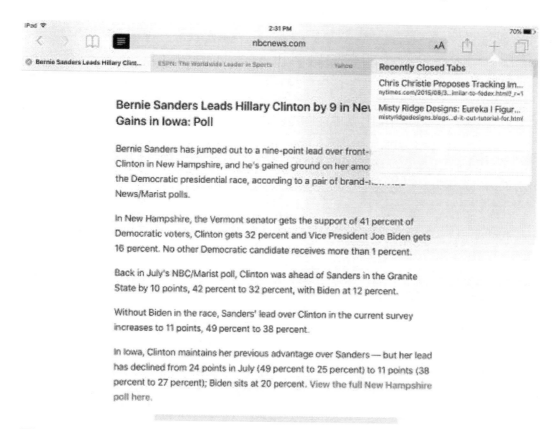 icon on the Home screen. The Safari Web browser opens.

2. Touch and hold the ✛ icon. A list of recently closed browser tabs appears, as shown in **Figure 12**.

3. Touch one of the websites in the list. The selected website opens in a new tab.

Figure 12: List of Recently Closed Tabs

13. Scanning a Credit Card Using the Device's Camera

When you wish to use a credit card to purchase a product online, you have the option to use your device's camera to scan the card. To scan a credit card using the camera:

1. Navigate to the website where you wish to enter the credit card number. Refer to *"Navigating to a Website"* on page 114 to learn how.
2. Touch the credit card field on the page. The virtual keyboard appears.
3. Touch **Scan Credit Card** above the keyboard. The camera turns on. If the Camera Access dialog appears, touch **OK** to allows Safari to use the camera.
4. Align the credit card with the white frame on the screen. The camera reads the credit card number, and enters it in the field.

Note: You will still need use the keyboard to enter the expiration date and security code (on the back of your card).

Managing Photos and Videos

Table of Contents

1.   Taking a Picture
2.   Capturing a Video
3.   Using the Digital Zoom
4.   Using the Flash (iPhone Only)
5.   Focusing on a Part of the Screen
6.   Browsing Photos
7.   Editing a Photo
8.   Deleting a Photo
9.   Creating a Photo Album
10. Editing a Photo Album
11. Deleting a Photo Album
12. Starting a Slideshow
13. Browsing Photos by Date and Location
14. Searching for a Photo
15. Recording a Time-Lapse Video
16. Recovering Deleted Photos
17. Using a Video Overlay to Watch a Video (Certain iPad Models Only)
18. Managing People in Photos
19. Managing Memories in Photos
20. Capturing and Viewing a Live Photo (iPhone 6S and Later Only)

1. Taking a Picture

iOS 10 devices have built-in rear-facing and front-facing cameras. To take a picture, touch the icon on the Home screen. The camera turns on, as shown in **Figure 1**. Use the following tips when taking a picture:

- Touch **Square** to take a square picture. Touch **Photo** to activate the default camera.
- Touch the button to switch between the cameras.

- Touch the ⬜ button to take a picture. The picture is captured, and is automatically stored on the device. If the surroundings are too dark and you are using an iPhone, refer to **Using the Flash** for help.

Note: Refer to "Tips and Tricks" *on page 293* *to learn how to take a picture directly from the Lock screen.*

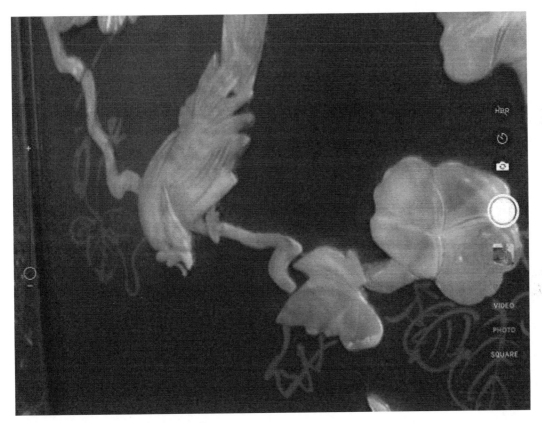

Figure 1: Camera Turned On

2. Capturing a Video

iOS 10 devices have a built-in camcorder that can shoot HD video. To capture a video:

1. Touch the 📷 icon. The camera turns on.
2. Touch **Video**. The camcorder turns on.
3. Touch the ⬜ button. The camera begins to record.

4. Touch the ⬤ button. The camera stops recording and the video is automatically saved to the 'Videos' album.

Note: Touch the thumbnail below the ⬤ or ⬤ button to preview the video.

3. Using the Digital Zoom

While taking pictures or capturing video, use the camera's built-in Digital Zoom feature if the subject of the photo is far away. To zoom in before taking a photo, touch the screen with two fingers and move them apart. The ▬━━━━◯━━━━╋ appears at the bottom of the screen, and the camera zooms in. To zoom out before taking a photo, touch the screen with two fingers apart and bring them together. The ▬━━━━◯━━━━╋ appears at the bottom of the screen, and the camera zooms out.

Note: Because of its digital nature, the zoom function will not provide the best resolution, and the image may look fuzzy. Try to be as close as possible to the subject of the photo.

4. Using the Flash (iPhone Only)

iPhones have a built-in LED flash that can be used along with the rear-facing camera. When shooting a video with the flash turned on, it will remain on throughout the movie. To use the flash:

1. Make sure the camera is turned on and the rear camera is activated. Refer to *"Taking a Picture"* on page 130 to learn how.
2. Touch the ⚡ icon in the upper-left hand corner of the screen. The ⚡**Auto   On   Off** menu appears.
3. Touch **On**. The flash is turned on and will be used when taking a picture or capturing a video.
4. Touch **Off.** The flash is turned off and will never be used.
5. Touch **Auto**. The flash will be used as needed, as determined by the device's light sensor.

Note: The camera on an iPad and the front-facing camera on an iPhone do not have a built-in flash.

5. Focusing on a Part of the Screen

While taking pictures, the camera can focus on a particular object or area on the screen. This will adjust the lighting and other elements to make the object or area stand out in the picture. To focus on a specific part of the screen, just touch that area. An orange box appears and the camera focuses.

6. Browsing Photos

After taking photos on your device or transferring them from your computer, you may view them at any time. To view saved photos:

1. Touch the ⬤ icon on the Home screen. The Photos application opens.
2. Touch **Albums** at the bottom of the screen. A list of photo albums appears, as shown in **Figure 2**.
3. Touch an album. The photos in the album appear.
4. Touch a photo. The photo appears in full screen.
5. Use the following tips when viewing photos:

   - Touch a photo with your thumb and forefinger and move the two fingers apart to zoom in on it. The zoom will center where your fingers were joined.
   - Touch the screen twice quickly to zoom out completely. Touch the photo with your thumb and forefinger spread apart and move the fingers together while touching the photo to zoom out gradually. Move your fingers apart to zoom in.

   - Touch the ＜ button at the top of the screen while viewing a photo to return to album view. If the ＜ button is not shown, touch the photo once to make the photo menus appear at the top and bottom of the screen.
   - Touch and hold the photo ribbon at the bottom of the screen. Slide your finger to the left or right to preview each photo. Release the screen to leave the current photo on the screen.
   - Touch the screen and slide your finger up while viewing a photo to see related photos. Related photos may contain the same people (using facial recognition) or be captured in the same location.

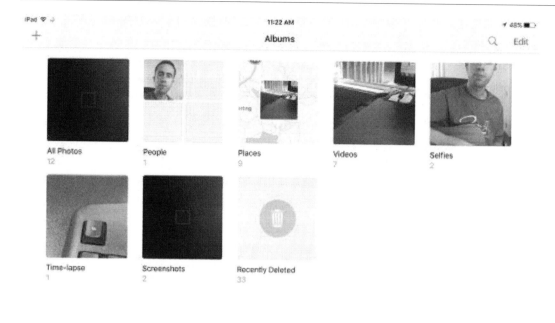

Figure 2: List of Photo Albums

7. Editing a Photo

iOS 10 provides advanced photo-editing tools. To edit a photo:

1. Touch the ![icon] icon at the Home screen. The Photos application opens.
2. Touch **Albums**. A list of photo albums appears.
3. Touch an album. The photos in the album appear.
4. Touch a photo. The photo appears in full screen.
5. Touch the ![icon] button at the top of the screen. The Photo Editing menu appears, as shown in **Figure 3**.
6. Touch one of the following icons to edit the photo:

- Enhances the quality of the photo. Touch **Done** to save the changes.

- Allows you to crop or rotate the photo. Touch the corners of the photo and drag the selected portion, as shown in **Figure 4**. Touch **Done** at the bottom of the screen to save the crop. Repeat steps 1-6 above, and touch **Revert** to return the photo to its original appearance.

- Allows you to add a color effect, such as Mono (grayscale) or Instant (Polaroid) to the photo. Touch the color effect to view a preview of the photo with the effect applied. Touch the same effect again to return to viewing the original.

- Allows you to customize the appearance of the photo by adjusting the amount of light, color, and tone in the photo. These settings are for advanced users only.

(Available only when a photo contains a face) - Removes red-eye from the photo. Touch each red eye in the photo and then touch **Done** to save the changes.

- Allows you to draw on, magnify parts of, or add text to a photo. Touch this icon, and then touch **Markup** to use this feature. The Markup screen appears, as shown in **Figure 5**. On the Markup screen, touch one of the following icons to perform the corresponding markup:

 - Doodle on the photo. Touch the icon to select the color of your pencil.

 - Magnify a portion of the photo.

 - Add text to a photo. Touch the ᴀA icon to change the font size and style.

Figure 3: Photo Editing Menu

Figure 4: Cropping a Photo

Figure 5: Markup Screen

8. Deleting a Photo

You may delete unwanted pictures from your device to free up memory. To delete a photo:
Warning: Once a picture is deleted, there is no way to restore it unless you have backed it up in
iTunes or iCloud. Deleting a picture removes it from all albums.

1. Touch the ![icon] icon. The Photos application opens.
2. Touch **Albums** at the bottom of the screen. A list of photo albums appears.
3. Touch an album. The photos contained in the album appear.
4. Touch a photo. The photo appears in full screen view.
5. Touch the ![trash] button. A confirmation dialog appears.
6. Touch **Delete Photo**. The photo is deleted from all albums on the device. You may also
   delete several pictures at a time, by touching **Select** at the top of an album, and then
   selecting each photo that you wish to delete. Follow steps 5-6 to delete the selected photos.

Note: Refer to "Recovering Deleted Photos" *on page 145 to learn how to recover deleted photos within 30 days of deleting them.*

9. Creating a Photo Album

You can create a photo album right on your device. To create a photo album:

1. Touch the ⚙ icon. The Photos application opens.
2. Touch **Albums** at the bottom of the screen. A list of photo albums appears.
3. Touch the ➕ button at the top of the screen. The New Album window appears, as shown in **Figure 6**.
4. Enter a name for the album and touch **Save**. The new photo album is created, and you can now choose photos to add to it.
5. Touch a photo album, and then touch photos to add them. Touch a photo a second time to deselect it. Touch **Albums** at the bottom of the screen at any time to return to the album list.
6. Touch **Done** at the top of the screen. The selected photos are added to the new photo album.

Figure 6: New Album Window

10. Editing a Photo Album

Photo albums stored on the device can be edited right from your device. Refer to **Creating a Photo Album** to learn how to make a new photo album using your device.

To edit the name of a photo album:

1. Touch the ⚘ icon. The Photos application opens.
2. Touch **Albums** at the bottom of the screen. A list of photo albums appears.

3. Touch **Edit** at the top of the screen. A ⊖ icon appears next to each album that may be edited. Albums that are on your device by default cannot be edited.
4. Touch the name of a photo album. The virtual keyboard appears.
5. Enter a new name for the album and touch **Done**. The album is renamed.

To add photos to an album:

1. Touch the ![flower icon] icon. The Photos application opens.
2. Touch **Albums** at the bottom of the screen. A list of photo albums appears.
3. Touch an album. The photos contained in the album appear.
4. Touch **Select** in the upper right-hand corner of the screen. Photos can now be selected.
5. Touch as many photos as desired. The photos are selected, and ![checkmark icon] icons appear on the thumbnails, as shown in **Figure 7**.
6. Touch **Add To**. A list of photo albums appears. You cannot add photos to any album that is grayed out.
7. Touch the name of a photo album. The selected photos are added to the album.

Note: Adding photos to an album does not remove them from the original album.

Figure 7: Selected Photos

11. Deleting a Photo Album

Photo albums stored on the device can be deleted right from your device. To delete a photo album:

Warning: When an album is deleted from the device, any photos that are stored in other albums will remain on the device. Make sure any photos you wish to keep are stored in another album. Refer to "Editing a Photo Album" on page 140 to learn how to add photos to an album.

1. Touch the ✹ icon. The Photos application opens.
2. Touch **Albums** at the bottom of the screen. A list of photo albums appears.

3. Touch **Edit** at the top of the screen. A ⊖ icon appears next to each album that may be deleted.

4. Touch the ⊖ icon next to an album. A confirmation dialog appears.
5. Touch **Delete**. The photo album is deleted.

12. Starting a Slideshow

The iOS 10 device can play a slideshow using the photos in your albums. To begin a slideshow:

1. Touch the ✹ icon. The Photos application opens.
2. Touch **Albums** at the bottom of the screen. A list of photo albums appears.
3. Touch an album. The photos in the album appear.
4. Touch **Slideshow** at the top of the screen. The Slideshow begins.
5. Touch the screen anywhere to pause the slideshow. Touch **Options** while the slideshow is paused to customize the slideshow settings.
6. Touch **Theme** and select the transition for the slideshow. You may also touch **Music** to select Music from your library.
7. Touch the ▶ button to resume the slideshow.

13. Browsing Photos by Date and Location

The device can sort photos according to the physical locations where they were taken, as well as the dates on which they were captured. To browse photos by date and location:

1. Touch the ![icon] icon. The Photos application opens.
2. Touch **Photos** at the bottom of the screen. The Moments screen appears.
3. Touch **Collections** at the top of the screen. A list of albums appears, organized by date and location, as shown in **Figure 8**.
4. Touch an album in any location. The selected album opens.
5. Touch the name of a town. A map appears, showing the locations where photos were taken. Touch **Moments** to return to the photo list.

Note: You may only view pictures sorted by location if you have Location Services turned on.
Refer to "Turning Location Services On or Off" on page 216 to learn more.

Figure 8: List of Albums Organized by Date and Location

14. Searching for a Photo

Use the Search feature to find a photo more quickly while viewing the Photos application. To search for a photo:

1. Touch the  icon at the top of the screen while using the Photos application. 'Search Photos' appears.
2. Enter the name of the album, or the location where the photo was taken. You may also search by date.
3. Touch **Search**. A list of matching results appears as you type, as shown in **Figure 9**.

Figure 9: List of Matching Photo Results

15. Recording a Time-Lapse Video

You can record a time-lapse video, which allows you to capture a short video of an event that takes place over a long period of time, such as the budding of a flower. To record a time-lapse video:

1. Touch the icon. The camera turns on.
2. Touch **Photo** and slide your finger down. Continue to do this until you see 'Time-Lapse'.
3. Touch **Time-Lapse**. The time-lapse camcorder turns on.
4. Touch the button. The camcorder begins to record the time-lapse video.
5. Touch the button. The time-lapse video is captured and stored in the 'Time-lapse' album. The Photos application marks every time-lapse video with the icon.

16. Recovering Deleted Photos

You may recover a deleted photo if fewer than 30 days have passed since you deleted it. To recover deleted photos:

1. Touch the icon. The Photos application opens.
2. Touch **Albums** at the bottom of the screen. A list of photo albums appears.
3. Touch the **Recently Deleted** album. The recently deleted photos appear. The number of days on each photo shows the amount of time left before the photo will be permanently deleted.
4. Touch **Select**, and then touch each photo that you want to recover. The photos are selected, and icons appear on the thumbnails.
5. Touch **Recover**. A confirmation dialog appears.
6. Touch **Recover Photo**. The selected photos are returned to their original albums.

17. Using a Video Overlay to Watch a Video (Certain iPad Models Only)

You can watch a video on your iPad while using another application or viewing the Home screen. This feature is known as Persistent Video Overlay. Only the following iPad models are compatible with Persistent Video Overlay:

- iPad Air
- iPad Air 2
- iPad mini 2
- iPad mini 3

To turn on Persistent Video Overlay:

1. Touch the ⊚ icon. The Settings screen appears.
2. Touch **General**. The General Settings screen appears.
3. Touch **Multitasking**. The Multitasking Settings screen appears.
4. Touch the ⬭ switch next to 'Persistent Video Overlay'. The ⬤ switch appears and Persistent Video Overlay is turned on. Turn the feature off by touching the ⬤ switch.

To use Persistent Video Overlay:

1. Touch the ⧐ icon, and select a video to play.
2. While the video is playing, touch the ⬚ icon. The video is minimized to a thumbnail.
3. Press the **Home** button. The video continues to play in a thumbnail, as shown in **Figure 10**.
4. Touch and hold the thumbnail, and drag it to any of the four corners of the screen. You can also drag it to the left or right edge of the screen to hide it. Touch the black arrow to reopen the thumbnail.
5. Touch the thumbnail to view the video controls. Use the following controls to control the video:

❚❚ - Pause the video.

▶ - Resume playback.

✕ - Close the video thumbnail. The video stops playing.

↖▬ - Open the video in the Videos application.

Figure 10: Video Thumbnail

18. Managing People in Photos

The Photos application recognizes faces to place groups of photos in the People album when they contain the same person. When you use your device for the first time, it may take some time to process your photos, but it should pick up faces more quickly when you add them in the future. To manage people in Photos:

1. Touch the ✴ icon. The Photos application opens.
2. Touch **Albums** at the bottom of the screen. A list of photo albums appears.
3. Touch the **People** album. The People album opens, as shown in **Figure 11**.
4. Use the following tips when managing the People album:
    - Touch and hold a person in the list, and then drag it to the Favorites bar to add the person to your Favorites.
    - Touch a person's face to view all pictures that include that person.
    - While viewing a person's pictures, scroll down to the bottom, and then touch **Add to Memories** to include the person in your memories. Refer to *"Managing Memories in Photos"* on page 149 to learn more about Memories in Photos.
    - To hide a person from the list, touch **Select**, and then touch each person that you wish to hide. Touch **Hide**. You can always show the people that you have hidden by touching **Show Hidden People**.

Figure 11: People Album

19. Managing Memories in Photos

The Memories folder also uses the facial recognition feature to create photo arrangements. After there are a sufficient number of pictures or videos on your device, touch **Memories** at the bottom of the screen in the Photos application to view your memories.

20. Capturing and Viewing a Live Photo (iPhone 6S and Later Only)

The iPhone 6S and any other iPhone with 3D Touch can take Live photos, which are animated photos that capture video several moments before and after the photo is captured. To capture a Live photo:

1. Make sure that the Live feature is turned on. Touch the icon at the top of the screen. The icon appears to indicate that Live is turned on, as outlined in **Figure 12**.

2. Touch the button. 'LIVE' appears at the top of the screen, and a Live photo is captured.

3. To view the Live photo, open the Photos application, and press the photo firmly. The animated photo plays.

Figure 12: Live Feature Turned On

Using iTunes

Table of Contents

1. Registering with Apple
2. Buying Music and Ringtones in iTunes
3. Buying or Renting Videos in iTunes
4. Searching for Media in iTunes
5. Playing Media
6. Sharing Your iTunes Account with Family

1. Registering with Apple

In order to buy content, you will need to have an iTunes account. Refer to *"Signing In to an iTunes Account"* on page 188 to learn more.

2. Buying Music and Ringtones in iTunes

Music and ringtones can be purchased directly from the device via iTunes. To buy music using the iTunes application:

1. Touch the ![icon] icon. The iTunes application opens.
2. Touch the ![icon] icon. The iTunes Music Store opens and the new releases are shown.
3. Touch **Genres** at the top of the screen to browse music. A list of Genres appears. You may also search for a specific song or artist by touching **Search** (iPad) or the ![search] button (iPhone).
4. Touch an album. The Album description appears, as shown in **Figure 1**.
5. Touch the price of the album. 'Buy Album' appears.
6. Touch **Buy Album**. The album is purchased. Touch the price of a song and then touch **Buy Song** to buy a single song.
7. To purchase a ringtone, follow steps 1-3, and then touch the name of the ringtone. Touch **Buy** to purchase the ringtone.

Note: You may need to enter your iTunes password when purchasing music on the device.

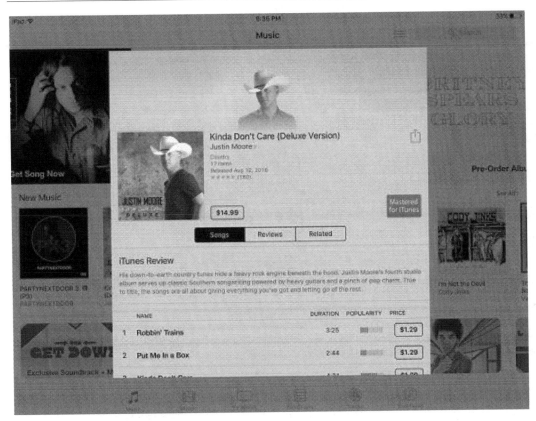

Figure 1: Album Description

3. Buying or Renting Videos in iTunes

Videos can be purchased or rented directly from the device and viewed using the Music application. To buy videos using the iTunes application:

1. Touch the [icon] icon. The iTunes application opens.
2. Touch the [icon] icon or the [icon] icon. The iTunes Video Store opens, and the featured videos appear, as shown in **Figure 2** (Movie Store).
3. Touch a video. The Video description appears, as shown in **Figure 3**.
4. Touch the price of the video. 'Buy Movie', 'Rent Movie', or 'Buy HD Episode' appears, depending on your selection.
5. Touch **Buy NAME**, where NAME refers to the type of video that you are buying. The device may ask for your iTunes password. The video is purchased or rented, and the download begins.

Note: When renting a video, the video is available for 24 hours once you start watching it. Once 24 hours has passed, you will not be able to resume the video if you pause it.

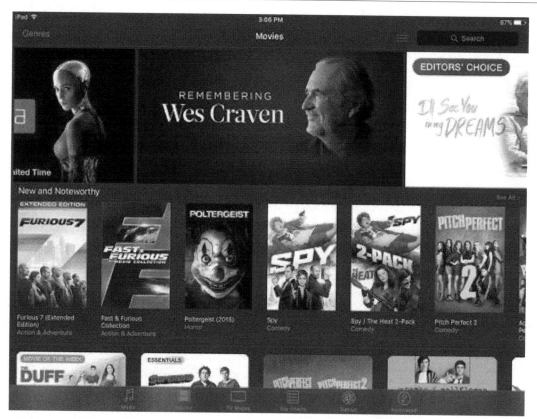

Figure 2: iTunes Video Store (Movies)

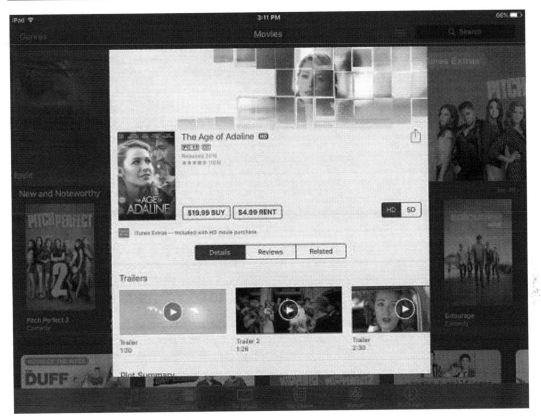

Figure 3: Video Description

4. Searching for Media in iTunes

The device can search for any media in the iTunes Store. To search for media:

1. Touch the ![icon] icon. The iTunes application opens.
2. Touch the ![icon] icon. 'Search' appears at the top of the screen. Touch the ![button] button to clear the field, if necessary.
3. Enter the name of an artist, actor, song, or video that you wish to find. Touch **Search**. The matching results appear, organized by the type of media, as shown in **Figure 4**.
4. Touch a song, video, or ringtone. The media description appears.

Note: Refer to "Buying Music and Ringtones in iTunes" *on page 152 or* "Buying or Renting Videos in iTunes" *on page 153 to learn how to purchase media.*

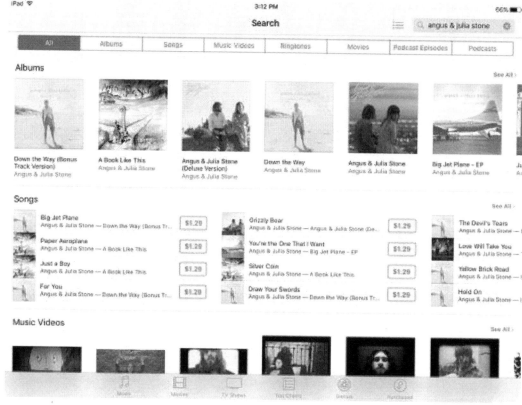

Figure 4: Available Media Results

5. Playing Media

To play media purchased in iTunes on the device, use the Music Application. To learn how, refer to *"Using the Music Application"* on page 158.

6. Sharing Your iTunes Account with Family

You may allow your friends or family members to purchase content using your iTunes account. Make sure that you trust the people to whom you give access to your iTunes account. To share your iTunes account:

1. Touch the icon. The Settings screen appears, as shown in **Figure 5**.
2. Scroll down and touch **iCloud**. The iCloud Settings appear.
3. Touch **Set Up Family Sharing**. The Family Sharing window appears.
4. Touch **Get Started**. The Family Setup begins.

5. Touch **Continue**. The Purchase Sharing screen appears.

6. Touch **Continue**. The Terms and Conditions appear.

7. Touch **Agree**, and then touch **Agree** again. The Payment Method screen appears.

8. Confirm that your payment method is correct, and touch **Continue**. The Location Sharing screen appears.

9. Touch **Share Your Location** to allow your family members or friends to view your location at all times, or touch **Not Now** to keep your location private. The Family settings appear.

10. Touch **Add Family Member**. The Add Family Member dialog appears.

11. Enter the name or email address of the family member or friend, and touch **Next**. An invitation to use your iTunes account is sent, and your contact may now use your account.

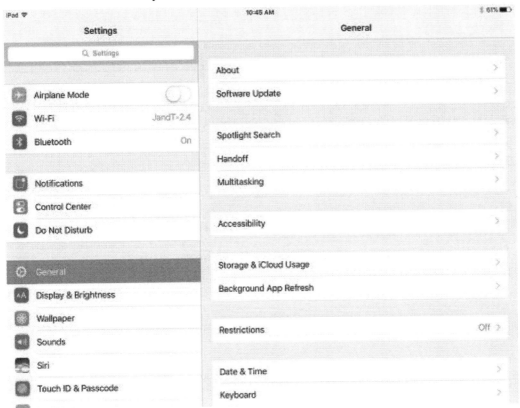

Figure 5: Settings Screen

Using the Music Application

Table of Contents

1. Downloading Media
2. Playing Music
3. Using Additional Audio Controls
4. Creating a Playlist
5. Using the iTunes Radio

1. Downloading Media

Use the iTunes Application to download media to the device. Refer to *"Using iTunes"* on page 152 to learn how.

2. Playing Music

The Music application on the device can be used to play music. To listen to your music:

1. Touch the ♫ icon. The Music application opens.
2. Touch **Library**, and then touch one of the following options to browse existing music:

   - Playlists
   - Artists
   - Albums
   - Songs
   - Downloaded Music

3. Use the following tips to navigate the Music Application:

- Touch a playlist, artist, or album to view the songs that the category contains. Touch a song to play the item. The item plays, as shown in **Figure 1**.
- After you have exited the Music application, touch the screen at the bottom and drag your finger up. The Control Center opens. Drag your finger to the right to bring up the music controls, as shown in **Figure 2**. Touch the name of the artist to return to the Music application.
- The music controls also appear on the lock screen, as shown in **Figure 3**.

Figure 1: Music Playing

Figure 2: Music Controls

Figure 3: Music Controls on the Lock Screen

3. Using Additional Audio Controls

Use the Song Controls to control music while it is playing. Touch one of the following to perform the corresponding function:

◄◄ - Skip to the beginning of the current song or skip to the previous song.

►► - Skip to the next song.

❚❚ - Pause the current song.

▶ - Resume the current song when it is paused.

↻ - Repeat the song or artist that is currently playing.

⸺ - Drag the ❘ on the bar at the top of the screen to go to a different part of the song.

- Shuffle all songs in the playlist. Touch again to play the songs in order.

*Note: Touch both **Repeat** and **Shuffle** to play songs continuously in random order. To shuffle and play all songs on the device, go to the song list and touch **Shuffle**.*

4. Creating a Playlist

Playlists can be created in iTunes. However, the Music application can perform the same function. To create a playlist in the Music application:

1. Touch **Library**, and then touch Playlists. The existing playlists appear.
2. Touch **New**. The New Playlist window appears, as shown in **Figure 4**.
3. Touch **Playlist Name**, and enter the name of the playlist.
4. Touch **Add Music**. A list of music categories on your phone appears, as shown in **Figure 5**.
5. Touch one of the categories to browse music to add to the new playlist.
6. Touch a song. A check mark appears next to each song that is added to the playlist.
7. Touch **Done**. The playlist is populated with the selected music.
8. Touch **Done**. The playlist is saved.

After creating a playlist, you can add or remove music from it. To edit a playlist:

1. Touch **Playlists** in the Music application. The existing playlists appear.
2. Touch a playlist. The Playlist screen appears, as shown in **Figure 6**.
3. Touch **Edit**. A ⊖ button appears next to every song in the playlist.
4. Touch the ⊖ button next to a song, and touch **Delete**. The song is removed from the playlist.
5. To add songs, touch **Add Music**, and then repeat steps 4 and 5 from the instructions above. The selected songs are added to the playlist.
6. Touch **Done**. The changes to the playlist are saved.

Note: Removing a song from a playlist will not delete it from the Music library.

Figure 4: New Playlist Window

Figure 5: List of Music Categories on Your Device

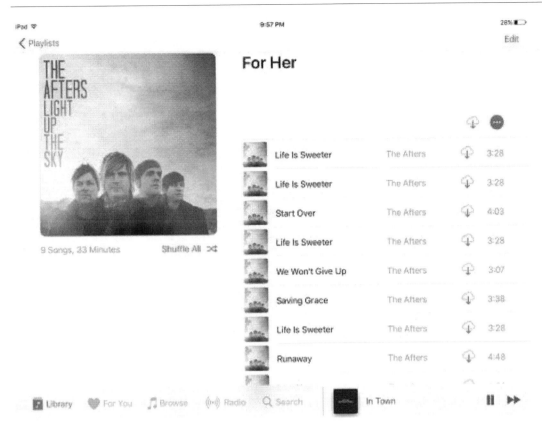

Figure 6: Playlist Screen

5. Using the iTunes Radio

The iTunes Radio is a free service that allows you to create personalized stations based on artists, songs, or genres.

To create a new iTunes Radio station, touch the ((•)) icon in the Music application. The iTunes Radio screen appears, as shown in **Figure 7**. Touch a genre in the list, or touch the search field at the top of the screen, and enter an artist, genre, or song. If you search for a station, touch the name of the artist, album, or song. The station begins to play, and is added to your list of stations automatically.

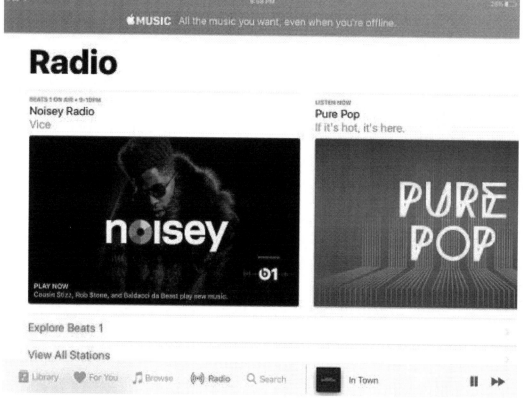

Figure 7: iTunes Radio Screen

Using the Mail Application

Table of Contents

1. Setting Up the Mail Application_
2. Reading Email
3. Switching Accounts in the Mail Application
4. Writing an Email
5. Referring to Another Email while Composing a New Message
6. Formatting Text
7. Replying to and Forwarding Emails
8. Attaching a Picture or Video to an Email
9. Moving an Email in the Inbox to Another Folder
10. Flagging an Important Email
11. Archiving Emails
12. Changing the Default Signature
13. Changing Email Options
14. Unsubscribing from an Email List
15. Viewing Emails in Conversation View

1. Setting Up the Mail application

Before the Mail application can be used, at least one account must be set up on your device. To set up the Mail application:

1. Touch the ⚙ icon. The Settings screen appears, as shown in **Figure 1**.
2. Scroll down and touch **Mail**. The Mail settings screen appears, as shown in **Figure 2**.
3. Touch **Accounts**. The Accounts screen appears, as shown in **Figure 3**.
4. Touch **Add Account**. The Account Type screen appears, as shown in **Figure 4**.
5. Touch one of the email services in the list to set up an email account. The corresponding email setup screen appears.
6. Enter all of the required information, and touch **Next** at the top of the screen. The Sync screen appears.
7. Select the types of content that you would like to sync from this account with your device, such as Mail, Contacts, or Calendars. Touch **Save**. The email account is added to your device.

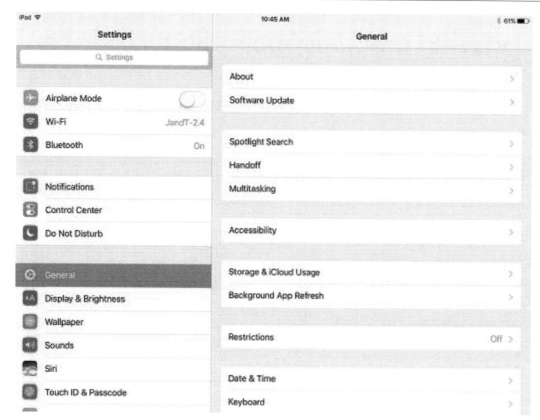

Figure 1: Settings Screen

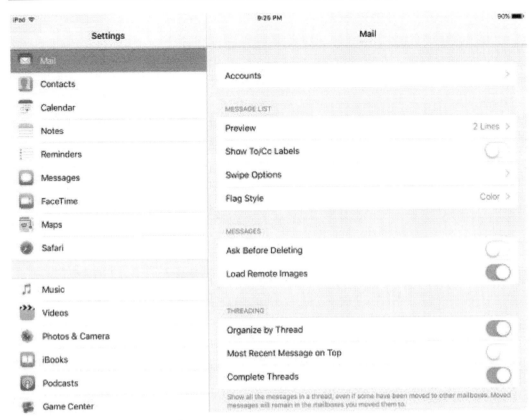

Figure 2: Mail Settings Screen

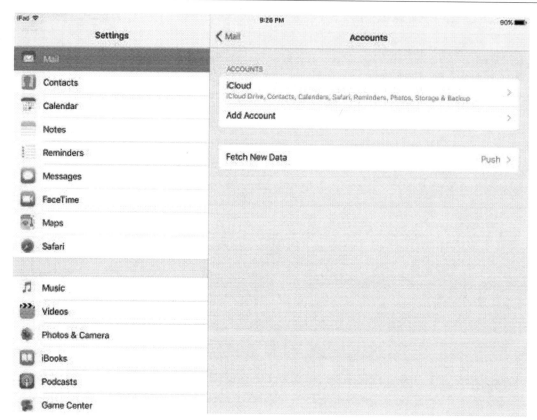

Figure 3: Accounts Screen

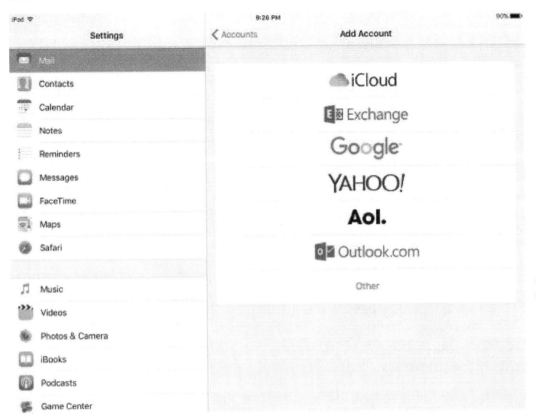

Figure 4: Account Type Screen

2. Reading Email

You can read your email on the device via the Mail application. Before opening the Mail application, make sure you have set up your email account. Refer to *"Setting Up the Mail Application"* on page 167 to learn how. To read your email:

1. Touch the ![icon] icon. The Mail application opens and the Inbox appears, as shown in **Figure 5**. If the emails are not shown, touch **Inbox** at the top of the screen.
2. Touch an email. The email opens.
3. Touch **Inbox** at the top of the screen in an email to return to the list of received emails (Portrait view only). Touch **Mailboxes** at the top of the Inbox to return to the list of mailboxes. The mailbox list varies depending on the email service.

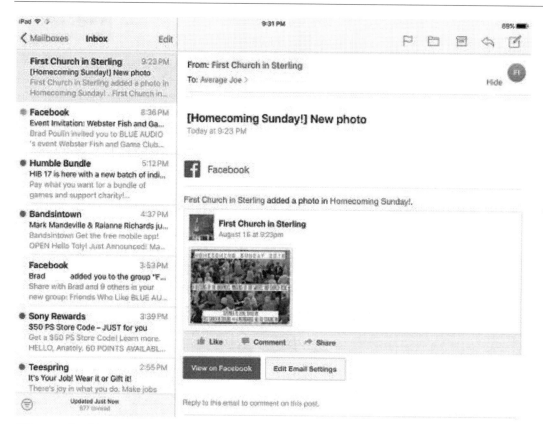

Figure 5: Email Inbox

3. Switching Accounts in the Mail application

If you have more than one active email account, you can switch between them, or view all of your email in one Inbox. To switch to another account:

1. Touch the ![icon] icon. The Mail application opens and your emails appear.
2. Touch **Mailboxes** at the top of the screen while viewing a list of messages in a folder. A list of all active inboxes and accounts appears, as shown in **Figure 6**.
3. Touch an account. The Inbox associated with the selected account appears.

You can also touch **All Inboxes** to view all emails from the accounts attached to your device in a single joint folder.

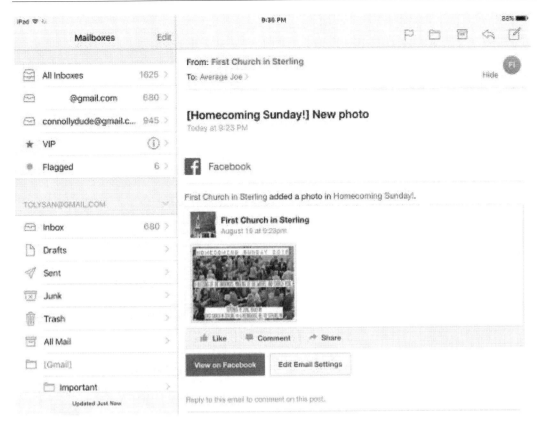

Figure 6: List of Active Inboxes and Accounts

4. Writing an Email

Compose email directly from the device using the Mail application. To write an email while using the Mail application:

1. Touch the 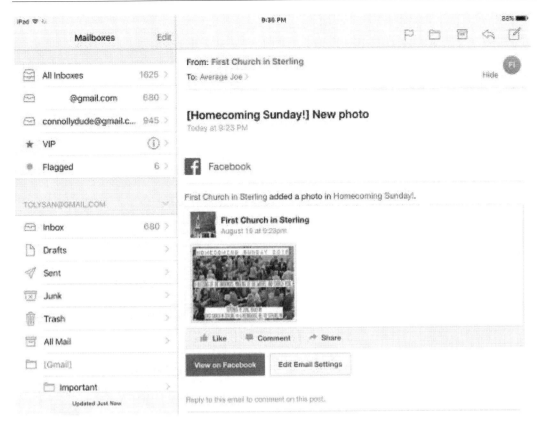 button. The New Email screen appears, as shown in **Figure 7**.
2. Start entering the name of a contact. A list of matching contacts appears as you type.
3. Touch the name of the contact that you wish to email. The contact's email address is added to the addressee list. Alternatively, enter an email address from scratch. Enter as many additional addressees as desired.
4. Touch the **return** key on the keyboard. The cursor jumps to the subject of the email. Enter a topic for the message.
5. Touch the **return** key on the keyboard. The cursor jumps to the body of the email. Enter the content of the email, and touch **Send** at the top of the screen. The email is sent.

Figure 7: New Email Screen

---

5. Referring to Another Email when Composing a New Message

While composing an email, you may wish to refer to another message for reference. To do so, touch the top of the **New Message** window, and drag your finger to the bottom of the screen. The New Message window is hidden, and you may use the Mail application normally. To continue writing your email where you left off, touch **New Message** at the bottom of the screen. If you have already entered a subject, 'New Message' is replaced by the subject.

6. Formatting Text

When writing an email on your device, you can format the text to add bold, italics, underline, or increase the quote level.

To add bold, italics, or underline text while writing an email:
1. Touch and hold the text in the email that you wish to format. The Select menu appears above the text, as shown in **Figure 8**.
2. Touch **Select All**. All of the text is selected. To select a single word, touch **Select**. Blue dots appear around the word or phrase.
3. Touch and hold one of the blue dots and drag it in any direction. The text between the dots is highlighted and a Text menu appears, as shown in **Figure 9**.
4. Touch the [B I U] button. 'Bold', 'Italics', and 'Underline' appear. If you do not see [B I U] button, touch the [▶] button in the Text menu.
5. Touch one of the formatting options. The associated formatting is applied to the selected text.

You can also increase the left margin, or quote level, in an email. To increase the quote level:

1. Touch and hold any location in your email. The text cursor flashes in the selected location.
2. Touch the [▶] button in the Text menu. The Text Format menu appears. This step only applies to the iPhone. If you are using an iPad, proceed to step 3.
3. Touch **Quote Level**. The Quote Level options appear.
4. Touch **Decrease** or **Increase** to adjust the Quote Level accordingly. The new Quote Level is set and applied to the paragraph where the text cursor is currently flashing.

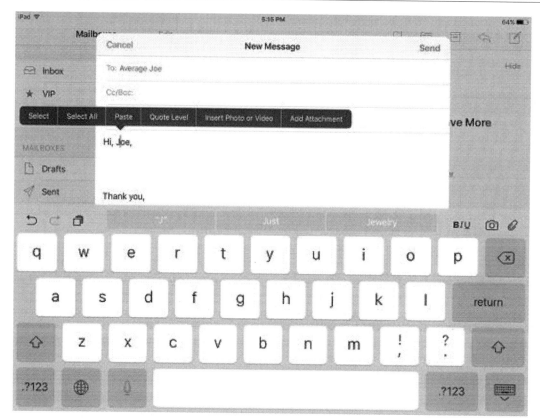

Figure 8: Select Menu

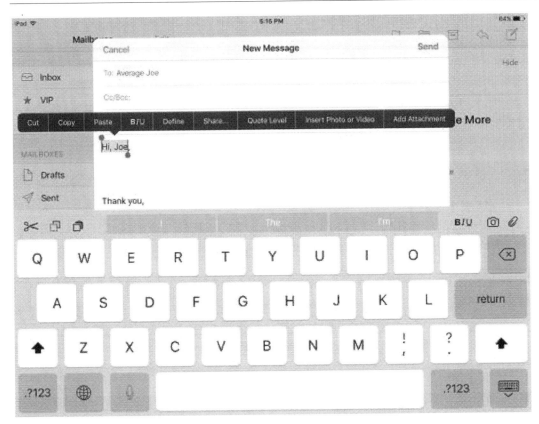

Figure 9: Text Menu

7. Replying to and Forwarding Email Messages

After receiving an email, you can reply to the sender or forward the email to a new recipient. To reply to, or forward an email:

1. Touch the ✉ icon. The Mail application opens.
2. Touch an email. The email appears.
3. Touch the ↩ button. The Reply menu appears, as shown in **Figure 10**.
4. Touch **Reply** to reply to the message, or touch **Forward** to forward the message. The New Message screen appears. The subject at the top is preceded by 'Re:' if replying, or 'Fwd:' if forwarding. The original email is copied in the body. If replying, the addressee field is filled in.
5. Touch the text field next to 'To:', and enter an addressee, if necessary. The addressee is entered. The address of the sender is automatically entered when replying to an email.
6. Touch the text field to the right of 'Subject' to enter a different subject for your message, if desired. The subject is entered.

7. Touch the text field below 'Subject' and enter a message, if desired. The message is entered.

8. Touch **Send** at the top of the screen. The email is sent.

*Note: When forwarding an email, the attachment menu will appear if the original message has an attachment. Touch **Include** if you wish to include the attachment when you forward the email. Otherwise, touch **Don't Include**.*

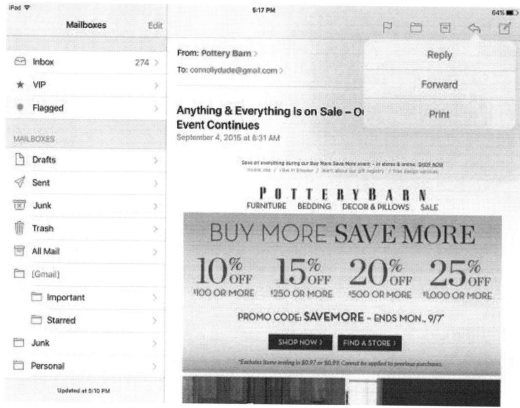

Figure 10: Reply Menu

8. Attaching a Picture or Video to an Email

While composing an email, you may wish to attach a picture or video to send to the recipient. To attach a picture or video to an email:

1. Touch and hold anywhere in the content of the email. The Select menu appears above the text.

2. Touch the ▶ button in the Select menu (iPhone only), and then touch **Insert Photo or Video**. On an iPad, immediately touch **Insert Photo or Video**. A list of photo albums stored on your device appears, as shown in **Figure 11**.
3. Touch the photo album that contains the photo that you wish to attach. The photo album opens and a list of photo thumbnails appears, as shown in **Figure 12**.
4. Touch the photo that you wish to attach. A preview of the photo appears.
5. Touch **Use**. The selected photo is attached. Alternatively, touch **Cancel** to return to the list of photos.

You can also attach several photos or videos at a time by viewing a photo in the Photos application, and touching the ⬆ icon. There is no limit to the number of photos that you can attach to an email when using an iPhone. However, the size of the email cannot exceed the limit set by your email provider. The five-photo limit still exists when attaching photos to an email using the iPad. Refer to *"Managing Photos and Videos"* on page 130 to learn more.

Note: You may move or delete the photo in the same way that you would delete text.

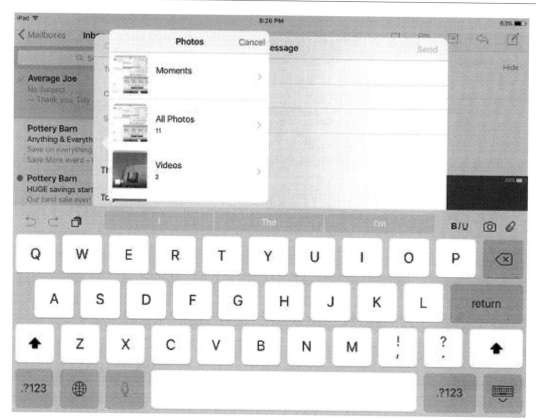

Figure 11: List of Photo Albums

Figure 12: List of Photo Thumbnails

9. Moving an Email in the Inbox to Another Folder

You may wish to organize emails into folders so that you can find them more easily. To move an email in the Inbox to another folder:

1. Touch an email in the Inbox. The email opens.
2. Touch the ⬜ button. A list of available folders appears, as shown in **Figure 13**.
3. Touch the name of a folder. The selected email is moved to the selected folder. To view a list of your folders, touch **Mailboxes** at the top of the screen while viewing the Inbox.

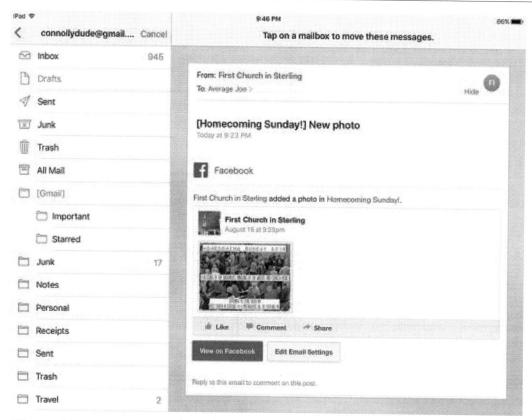

Figure 13: List of Available Folders

10. Flagging an Important Email

You may flag emails that are of the greatest importance in order to find them more quickly. This feature is especially useful if you do not have the time to read the email immediately, and wish to return to it in the near future. To flag an important email:

1. Touch an email in the Inbox. The email opens.

2. Touch the ⚑ button. The Flagging menu appears, as shown in **Figure 14**.

3. Touch **Flag**. The email is flagged as 'Important'. You may also touch **Mark as Unread** to flag the email so that you remember to read it later.

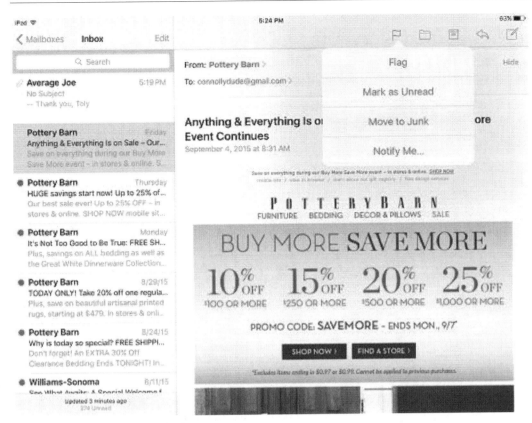

Figure 14: Flagging Menu

11. Archiving Emails

You may archive emails from your Inbox to free up space and improve organization. Archiving emails moves them to a folder that does not take up space on your device. Therefore, you never need to delete an email, and can always recover it if you did not mean to delete it. You may archive as many emails as you like. To archive an email:

1. Touch the ✉ icon. The Mail application opens.
2. Touch and hold an email in the list and drag your finger to the left until the email disappears. The email is sent to the 'All Mail' folder, and disappears from the Inbox. You can also archive an email by touching the 🗄 icon while viewing an open email.
3. Touch **Mailboxes** at the top of the screen, and then touch **All Mail** to view all emails, including those that have been archived.

12. Changing the Default Signature

The device can set a default signature that will be attached to the end of each email that is sent from the device. To set or change this signature:

1. Touch the 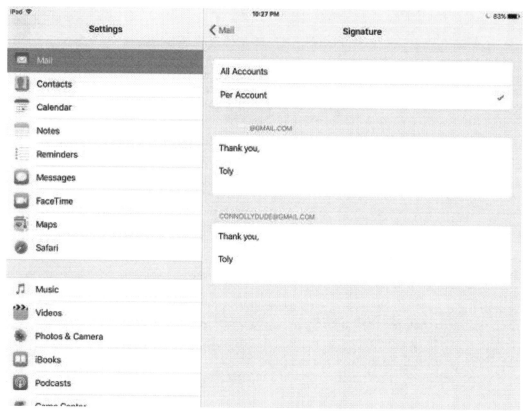 icon. The Settings screen appears.
2. Touch **Mail**. The Mail settings screen appears.
3. Scroll down and touch **Signature**. The Signature screen appears, as shown in **Figure 15**.
4. Enter a signature, and then touch **Mail** at the top of the screen. The new signature is saved.

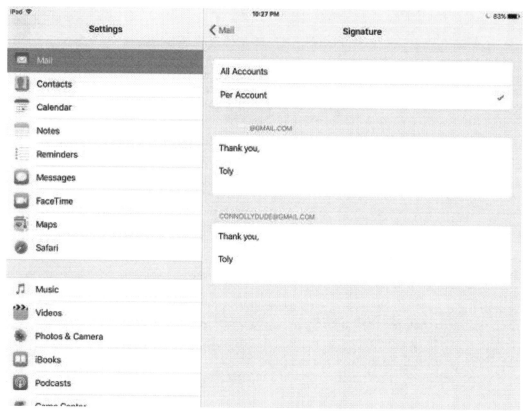

Figure 15: Signature Screen

13. Changing Email Options

There are various options that change the way your Mail application works. Touch the [icon] icon, and then touch **Mail** to change one of the following options:

- **Preview** - Choose the number of lines of an email message to preview in the Inbox.
- **Show To/Cc Label** - Choose whether to hide the 'To' and 'Cc' labels and show only addresses.
- **Swipe Options** - Changes the swipe action used to flag an email, or mark an email as 'Unread'.
- **Flag Style** - Choose the type of shape to use (color or shape) when flagging an email.
- **Ask Before Deleting** - Choose whether to display a confirmation before deleting an email.
- **Load Remote Images** - Choose whether to load images in an email automatically.
- **Organize by Thread** - Choose whether to group all emails with the same contact as a conversation.
- **Most Recent Message On Top** - Choose whether to always show the email that you received most recently at the top of a thread.
- **Complete Threads** - Choose whether to show an entire thread of emails with the same contact or group as a conversation even when you have moved some of the emails to other folders.
- **Always Bcc Myself** - Choose whether the Mail application sends a copy of each email to your own email address for your records.
- **Increase Quote Level** - Choose whether to increase the left margin when replying to or forwarding an email.

15. Unsubscribing from an Email List

You can now unsubscribe from mailing lists that crowd your inbox with unwanted emails. The Mail application automatically detects when an email is part of a mailing list. The following message appears at the top of the screen: "This message is from a mailing list."
Touch **Unsubscribe**. A confirmation dialog appears. Touch **Unsubscribe**. An email is sent on your behalf to remove you from the mailing list.

16. Viewing Emails in Conversation View

The Mail application lets you view email threads, or a list of emails that you have exchanged with a single contact or group, in the Inbox pane. If you have exchanged three or more emails with a contact or group, the ⟫ icon appears on the conversation in the Inbox pane, as outlined in **Figure 16**. Touch the ⟫ icon. The Conversation View appears, as shown in **Figure 17**. Touch the ⋁ icon to return to the normal Inbox view.

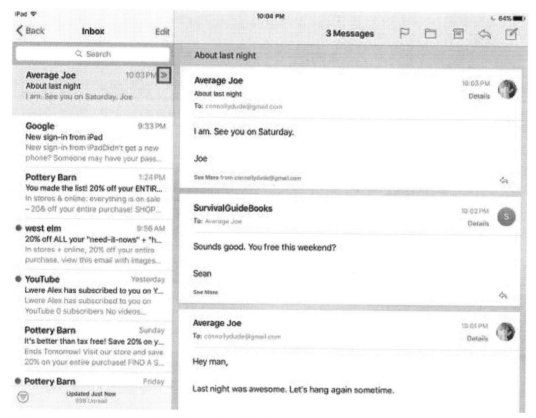

Figure 16: Conversation Icon Outlined

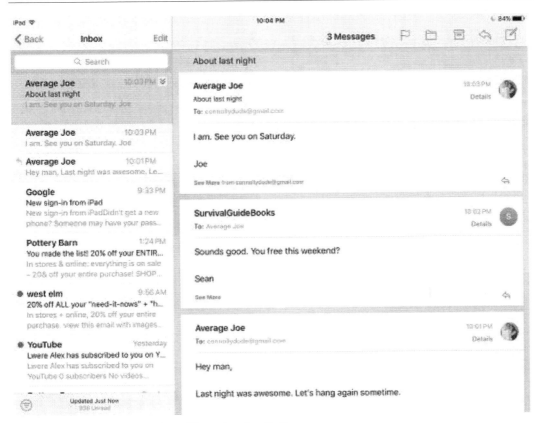

Figure 17: Conversation View in the Inbox

Managing Applications

Table of Contents

1. Signing In to an iTunes Account
2. Signing In to a Different iTunes Account
3. Editing iTunes Account Information
4. Searching for an Application to Purchase
5. Buying an Application
6. Using Wi-Fi to Download an Application
7. Switching Between Applications
8. Closing an Application Running in the Background
9. Organizing Applications into Folders
10. Reading User Reviews
11. Changing Application Settings
12. Deleting an Application
13. Sending an Application as a Gift
14. Redeeming a Gifted Application
15. Turning Automatic Application Updates On or Off
16. Using Slide Over to Multitask (Certain iPad Models Only)
17. Using Side-by-Side to Multitask (iPad Air 2 and Later Only)

1. Signing In to an iTunes Account

In order to buy applications, you will need to have an iTunes account. To set up a new iTunes account:

1. Touch the ![icon] icon. The Settings screen appears, as shown in **Figure 1**.
2. Scroll down and touch **iTunes & App Store**. The iTunes & App Stores screen appears, as shown in **Figure 2**.
3. Touch **Sign In**. If you already have an Apple ID, enter your Apple ID and password, and touch **Sign In** again. To register for an Apple ID, navigate to **https://appleid.apple.com/account** using your computer's Web browser.

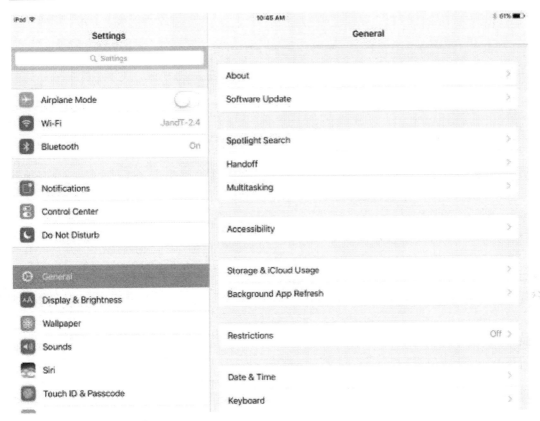

Figure 1: Settings Screen

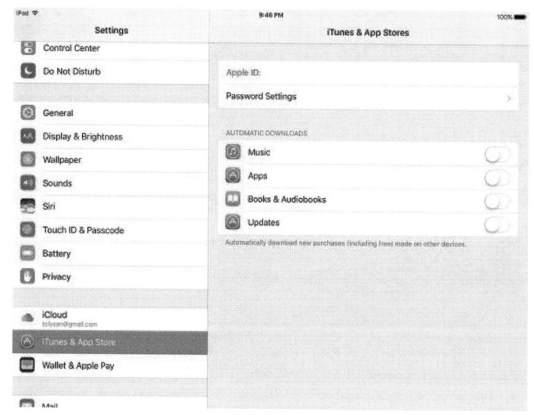

Figure 2: iTunes & App Stores screen

2. Signing In to a Different iTunes Account

If more than one person uses your device, you may wish to sign in with an alternate Apple ID. Only one Apple ID may be signed in at a time. To sign out and sign in to a different iTunes account:

1. Touch the ⊚ icon. The Settings screen appears.
2. Scroll down and touch **iTunes & App Store**. The iTunes & App Stores screen appears. If someone is signed in to their iTunes account on the device, their email appears at the top of the screen.
3. Touch the email address at the top of the screen. The Apple ID window appears, as shown in **Figure 3**.
4. Touch **Sign Out**. The account is signed out.
5. Touch **Sign In**. The virtual keyboard appears.
6. Enter your registered email address and password.

7. Touch **Sign In**. The account is signed in, and the owner's email is shown at the top of the iTunes & App Stores screen.

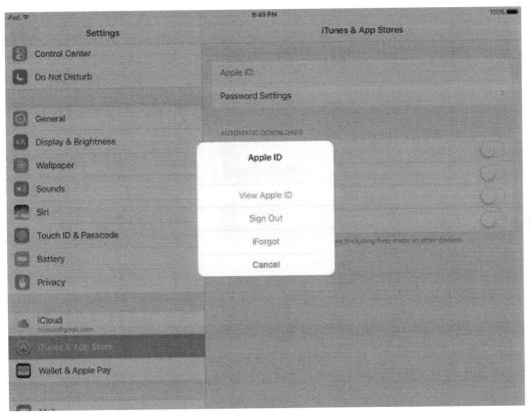

Figure 3: Apple ID Window

3. Editing iTunes Account Information

You must keep your account information up to date in order to purchase applications from the iTunes Application Store. For instance, when your billing address changes or your credit card expires, you must change your information. To edit iTunes account information:

1. Touch the ![icon] icon. The Settings screen appears.
2. Scroll down and touch **iTunes & App Store**. The iTunes & App Stores screen appears. If someone is signed in to their iTunes account on the device, their email appears at the top of the screen.
3. If you are not already signed in, enter your registered email and password, and touch **Done**. You are signed in.
4. Touch your email at the top of the screen. The Apple ID window appears.

5. Touch **View Apple ID**. The Account Settings screen appears with your personal account information.

6. Touch a field to edit it, and then touch **Done**. The new information is saved.

4. Searching for an Application to Purchase

Use the Application Store to search for applications. There are three ways to search for applications:

Manual Search

To search for an application manually:

1. Touch the icon. The Application Store opens, as shown in **Figure 4**.

2. Touch the field. The virtual keyboard appears and the search field is activated, as shown in **Figure 5**.

3. Enter the name of an application and touch **Search**. A list of matching results appears.

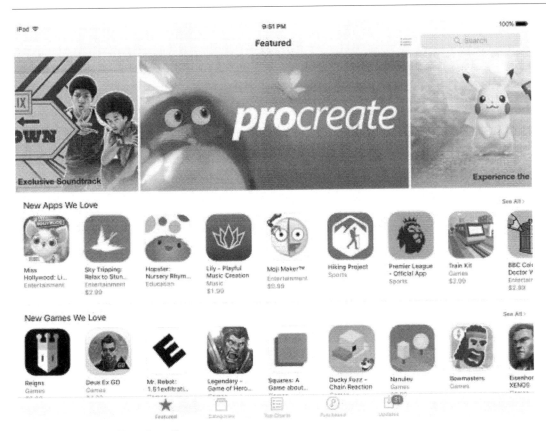

Figure 4: Application Store

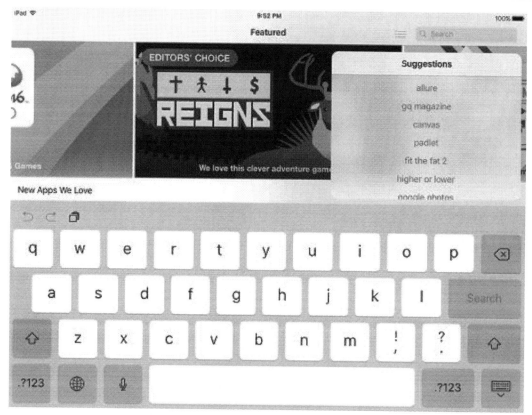

Figure 5: Search Field in the Application Store

Browse by Category

To browse applications by category:

1. Touch the icon. The Application Store opens.
2. Touch **Categories**. The Categories screen appears, as shown in **Figure 6**. Touch the screen and move your finger up or down to scroll through the categories.
3. Touch a category to browse it. Some categories have sub-categories. Repeat step 2 to find the sub-category that you need.

Figure 6: Categories Screen

Browse by Popularity

To browse applications by popularity:

1. Touch the icon. The Application Store opens.
2. Touch **Top Charts**. The Top Charts screen appears, as shown in **Figure 7**.
3. Touch one of the following to browse applications:
   - **Paid** - View the most popular paid applications.
   - **Free** - View the most popular free applications.
   - **Top Grossing** - View the most popular applications that have earned their creators the most money. Some Top Grossing apps are free, but in-app purchases are considered when calculating the top grossing applications.

Figure 7: Top Charts Screen

5. Buying an Application

You may purchase applications directly from your device. To buy an application:

1. Touch the icon. The Application Store opens.
2. Find an application. Refer to *"Searching for an Application to Purchase"* on page 192 to learn how.
3. Touch an application in the list. The Application description appears, as shown in **Figure 8**.
4. Touch the price of the application, or touch the word **FREE**, next to the name of the application. 'BUY' appears if the application is paid or 'INSTALL' if the application is free. If the application is already downloaded to your device, 'INSTALLED' or 'UPDATE' appears, depending on whether you require an update. Touch **BUY** or **INSTALL**. The password prompt appears.
5. Enter your iTunes password and touch **OK**. The device returns to the Home screen, and the application is downloaded and installed.

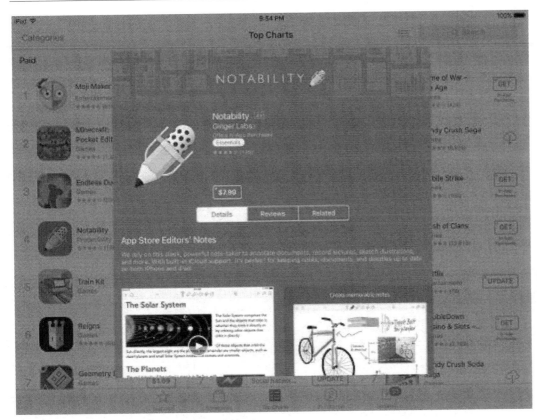

Figure 8: Application Description

6. Using Wi-Fi to Download an Application

Applications that are over 10MB in size require the device to be connected to a Wi-Fi network to download. These applications will display the following message: "Application over 10MB. Connect to a Wi-Fi network or use iTunes on your computer to download >APP NAME<'", where APP NAME refers to the name of the application you are trying to download. Refer to *"Using Wi-Fi"* on page 40 to learn how to turn on Wi-Fi.

7. Switching Between Applications

The device allows you to switch between running applications without having to exit any of them. For instance, you can listen to Pandora radio and read an eBook at the same time. To switch between applications:

1. Touch an application icon on one of your Home screens. The application opens.
2. Press the **Home** button. The Home screen is shown.
3. Open another application.
4. Press the **Home** button twice quickly. All of the open applications are displayed, as shown in **Figure 9**.
5. Touch an application icon. The device switches to the selected application.

When you open an application from inside another one, such as when you click a link in an email, a Back button appears in the upper left-hand corner of the screen. In the example of the email link, **Back to Mail** appears. Touch the Back button to return to the corresponding application.

Note: When switching to another application, the first application is never automatically closed. The application is simply running in the background. Refer to *"Closing an Application Running in the Background"* on page 199 to learn how to close an application.

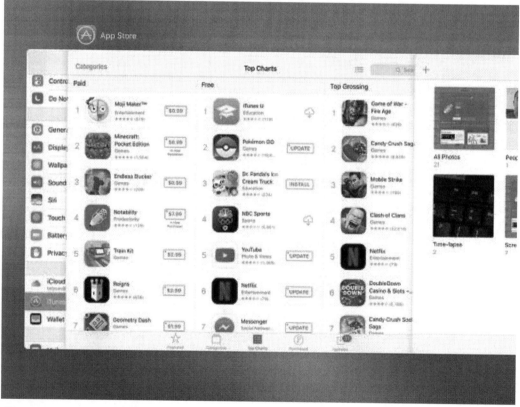

Figure 9: Open Applications

8. Closing an Application Running in the Background

After pressing the Home button to exit an application, it is not closed, but is left running in the background instead. It is good to have the application running because you can always switch to it quickly. However, if an application stops responding or if your battery is dying too quickly, you may wish to close it. To close an application running in the background, press the **Home** button twice quickly. All of the open applications are displayed. Touch and hold an application icon and slide your finger up. The application is closed. You can also close multiple applications at the same time by touching two or more applications and sliding your fingers up.

9. Organizing Applications into Folders

To learn how to organize applications into folders, refer to *"Creating an Icon Folder"* on page 39.

10. Reading User Reviews

In order to make a more informed decision when purchasing an application, you can read the reviews written by other users. However, be aware that people who have not used the application can also post reviews, which are uninformed. To read user reviews for an application:

1. Touch the ⬜ icon. The Application Store opens.
2. Find an application. Refer to *"Searching for an Application to Purchase"* on page 192 to learn how.
3. Touch an application icon. The Application description appears.
4. Touch **Reviews** below the name of the application. The reviews for the application appear.

11. Changing Application Settings

Some applications have settings that can be changed from the Settings screen. To change the application settings, touch the ⬜ icon. The Settings screen appears. Touch an application below 'Game Center' at the bottom of the screen. The Application Settings screen appears. The settings on this screen depend on the particular application.

12. Deleting an Application

You may delete most applications from your device to free up space on your memory card or Home screen. To delete an unwanted application:

1. Touch and hold an application icon. All of the applications on the Home screen begin to shake. Applications that can be erased have an ✕ button in their top left corner.

2. Touch the ✕ button next to an application icon. A confirmation dialog appears.
3. Touch **Delete**. The application is deleted.

4. Press the **Home** button. The application icons stop shaking and the ✕ buttons disappear.

Note: If you delete a paid application, you can download it again free of charge at any time. Refer to "Buying an Application" on page 196, and follow the instructions for buying the application to re-download it.

13. Sending an Application as a Gift

Applications can be sent as gifts. The recipient receives an email notification and can then download the gifted application from the Application Store. To send an application as a gift:

1. Touch the Ⓐ icon. The Application Store opens.
2. Find the application that you want to give as a gift. Refer to *"Searching for an Application to Purchase"* on page 192 to learn how.
3. Touch the application icon. The application description appears.

4. Touch the ⬆ icon. The Application options appear, as shown in **Figure 10**.
5. Touch **Gift**. The Send Gift screen appears, as shown in **Figure 11**.
6. Touch **To:** and enter the email address of the recipient of the gift. Enter an optional message.
7. Touch **Today** to select when the gift should be shared, if the date is other than the current day.
8. Touch **Next** at the top of the screen. The Theme Selection screen appears.

9. Select a theme and touch **Next** at the top of the screen. The Gift Confirmation screen appears, as shown in **Figure 12**.

10. Touch **Buy** at the top of the screen. 'BUY NOW' appears as a confirmation.

11. Touch **BUY NOW**. The password prompt appears.

12. Enter your iTunes password and touch **OK**. The gift is purchased and sent.

Note: You are charged for the gifted application as soon as you purchase it.

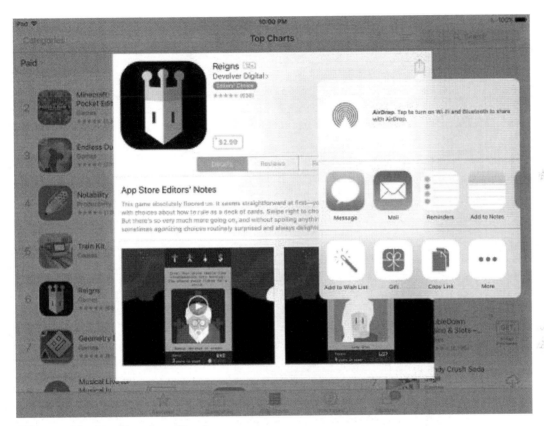

Figure 10: Application Options

Figure 11: Send Gift Screen

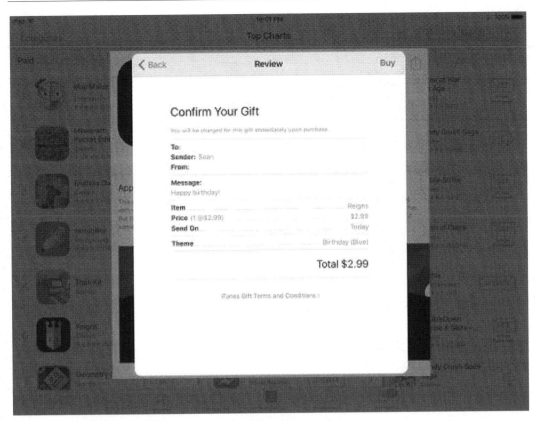

Figure 12: Gift Confirmation Screen

14. Redeeming a Gifted Application

When receiving an application as a gift, you must redeem it in order to download it. To redeem a gift and download the application using your device:

1. Touch the 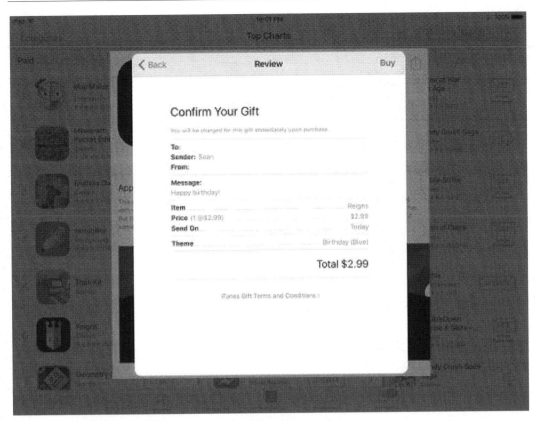 icon. The email application opens.
2. Touch the email with the subject '**NAME sent you an iTunes Gift**', where NAME represents the name of the sender. The email opens. Refer to *"Reading Email"* on page 171 to learn how to find an email.
3. Touch the **Redeem Now** button in the email. The Application Store opens.
4. Touch **Redeem** at the top of the screen. The gifted application is downloaded and installed. If the application is over 10MB, you must first turn on Wi-Fi. Refer to *"Using Wi-Fi"* on page 40 to learn how to turn Wi-Fi on. If this is your first time downloading an application from the iTunes store, you will need to touch **Agree** several times to accept several pages of terms and conditions.

15. Turning Automatic Application Updates On or Off

The device can automatically download updates for applications when new versions are released. To turn automatic application updates on or off:

1. Touch the 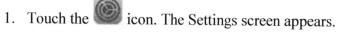 icon. The Settings screen appears.
2. Scroll down and touch **iTunes & App Store**. The iTunes & App Stores screen appears.
3. Touch the switch next to 'Updates' under 'Automatic Downloads'. The switch appears and Automatic application updates are turned off.
4. Touch the switch next to 'Updates' under 'Automatic Downloads'. The switch appears and Automatic application updates are turned on.

16. Using Slide Over to Multitask (Certain iPad Models Only)

You can reference an application while using another by opening a second application on the right side of the screen. Most applications are compatible with this feature, which is called Slide Over. In addition, only the following iPad models are compatible with Slide Over:

- iPad Air
- iPad Air 2
- iPad mini 2
- iPad mini 3
- Future iPad Models

To use slide over, turn on the feature first. To turn on slide over:

1. Touch the icon. The Settings screen appears.
2. Touch **General**. The General Settings screen appears, as shown in **Figure 13**.
3. Touch **Multitasking**. The Multitasking Settings screen appears, as shown in **Figure 14**.
4. Touch the switch next to 'Allow Multiple Apps'. The switch appears and Slide Over is turned on. Turn the feature off by touching the switch.

To use slide over:

1. Touch the right-hand side of the screen in the center at any time, and slide your finger to the left. The Slide Over Application window appears, as shown in **Figure 15**.
2. Touch an application in the list. The application opens in the window on the right-hand side of the screen. Use the following tips when using Slide Over:
   - To select another application, touch the black stripe at the top of the window and slide your finger down. A list of applications appears.
   - To hide the Slide Over window, touch the screen anywhere outside of the window.

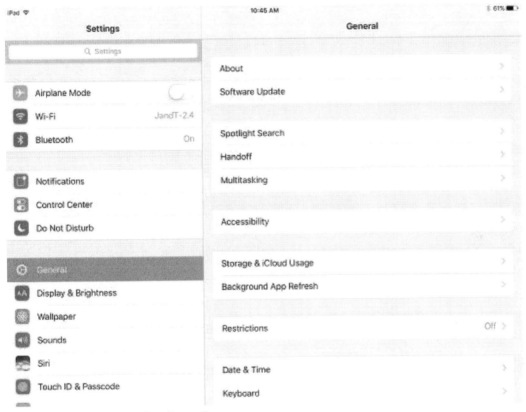

Figure 13: General Settings Screen

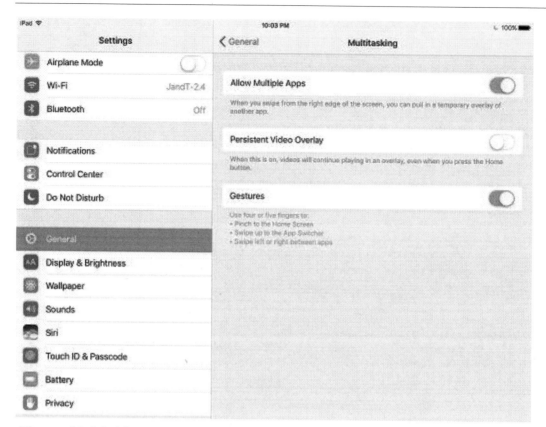

Figure 14: Multitasking Settings Screen

Figure 15: Slide Over Application Window

17. Using Side-by-Side to Multitask (iPad Air 2 and Later Only)

iOS 10 on the iPad Air 2 lets you use two applications on one screen, stacked side-by-side. Most applications are compatible with this feature. To use Side-by-Side to multitask, turn on this feature. To turn on Side-by-Side:

1. Touch the 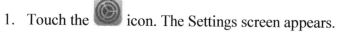 icon. The Settings screen appears.
2. Touch **General**. The General Settings screen appears.
3. Touch **Multitasking**. The Multitasking Settings screen appears.
4. Touch the ⬤ switch next to 'Allow Multiple Apps'. The ⬤ switch appears and

    Slide Over is turned on. Turn the feature off by touching the ⬤ switch.

To use side-by-side:

1. Touch the right-hand side of the screen at any time, and slide your finger to the left. The Slide Over Application window appears.
2. Touch an application in the list. The application opens in the window on the right-hand side of the screen.
3. Touch the white divider between the two applications and slide your finger to the left. The two applications appear side-by-side. To open one of the applications in full screen, touch the white divider, and slide your finger to the left or right.

Using Siri

Siri is a voice assistant that comes with every iOS 10 device. Follow the tips in this chapter to use Siri to its full potential.

Table of Contents

1. **Making a Call Using Siri**
2. **Sending and Receiving Text Messages Using Siri**
3. **Managing the Address Book Using Siri**
4. **Setting Up and Managing Meetings Using Siri**
5. **Checking the Time and Setting Alarms Using Siri**
6. **Sending and Receiving Email Using Siri**
7. **Getting Directions and Finding Businesses Using Siri**
8. **Playing Music Using Siri**
9. **Searching the Web and Asking Questions Using Siri**
10. **Looking Up Words in the Dictionary Using Siri**
11. **Application-Specific Phrases for Siri**

1. Making a Call Using Siri

To make a call using Siri, press and hold the **Home** button or hold the phone up to your ear and wait for Siri to speak (Siri does not speak when activated on some models). Say one of the following phrases:

- **Call John** (use any name)
- **Call Suzy Mobile**
- **Call Dexter on his work phone**
- **Call 123 555 1345**
- **Call home**
- **FaceTime Jacob**

Note: These phrases are only suggestions. Siri is flexible, and you can use many synonymous phrases.

2. Sending and Receiving Text Messages Using Siri

To send, read, or reply to a text message using Siri, press and hold the **Home** button or hold the phone up to your ear and wait for Siri to speak (Siri does not speak when activated on some models). Say one of the following phrases:

- Tell Anne See you soon
- Send a message to Rob Burr
- Send a message to Larry saying What's your address?
- Send a message to Julie on her mobile saying I got an device 6!
- Send a message to 999 555 2222
- Text Jude and Prudence What are you guys up to today?
- Read my new messages
- Read it again
- Reply that's great news
- Tell him ETA is 20 minutes
- Call her

Note: These phrases are only suggestions. Siri is flexible, and you can use many synonymous phrases.

3. Managing the Address Book Using Siri

To manage the address book using Siri, press and hold the **Home** button or hold the phone up to your ear and wait for Siri to speak (Siri does not speak when activated on some models). Say one of the following phrases:

- What's Joe's address?
- What is Susan Park's phone number?
- When is my grandfather's birthday?
- Show Bobby's email address
- Show Pete Abred
- Find people named Apple
- My brother is Trudy Ages (assigns a relationship to the name)
- Who is Colin Card? (indicates Colin Card's relationship to you)
- Call my brother at home (calls the number assigned to the relationship)

Note: These phrases are only suggestions. Siri is flexible, and you can use many synonymous phrases.

4. Setting Up and Managing Meetings Using Siri

To set up and manage meetings using Siri, press and hold the **Home** button or hold the phone up to your ear and wait for Siri to speak (Siri does not speak when activated on some models). Say one of the following phrases:

- Set up a meeting at 10
- Set up a meeting with Zoe at 9
- Meet with Nikki at noon
- New appointment with Dan Delion Tuesday at 4
- Schedule a focus group meeting at 3:30 today in the boardroom
- Move my 2pm meeting to 3:30
- Add Wendy to my meeting with Waldo
- Cancel the focus group meeting
- What does the rest of my day look like?
- What's on my calendar for Monday?
- When is my next appointment?
- Where is my next meeting?

Note: These phrases are only suggestions. Siri is flexible, and you can use many synonymous phrases.

5. Checking the Time and Setting Alarms Using Siri

To check the time and set alarms using Siri, press and hold the **Home** button or hold the phone up to your ear and wait for Siri to speak (Siri does not speak when activated on some models). Say one of the following phrases:

- Wake me up tomorrow at 6am
- Set an alarm for 6:30am
- Wake me up in 8 hours
- Change my 5:30 alarm to 6:30
- Turn off my 4:30 alarm
- What time is it?
- What time is it in Moscow?
- What is today's date?
- What's the date this Friday?
- Set the timer for 30 minutes
- Show the timer

- Pause the timer
- Resume
- Reset the timer
- Stop it

Note: These phrases are only suggestions. Siri is flexible, and you can use many synonymous phrases.

6. Sending and Receiving Email Using Siri

To send and receive email using Siri, press and hold the **Home** button or hold the phone up to your ear and wait for Siri to speak (Siri does not speak when activated on some models). Say one of the following phrases:

- Email Dave about the trip
- Email New email to John Diss
- Mail Dad about dinner
- Email Dr. Spaulding and say Got your message
- Mail Jack and Jill about the party and say It was awesome
- Check email
- Any new email from Mom today?
- Show new mail about the apartment
- Show the email from Roger yesterday
- Reply Dear Mark I'm sorry for your loss

Note: These phrases are only suggestions. Siri is flexible, and you can use many synonymous phrases.

7. Getting Directions and Finding Businesses Using Siri

To get directions and find businesses using Siri, press and hold the **Home** button or hold the phone up to your ear and wait for Siri to speak (Siri does not speak when activated on some models). Say one of the following phrases:

- How do I get home?
- Show 10 Park Ave. Boston Massachusetts
- Directions to my parents' home
- Find coffee near me

- Where is the closest Starbucks?
- Find a Mexican restaurant in New Mexico
- Find a gas station within walking distance

Note: These phrases are only suggestions. Siri is flexible, and you can use many synonymous phrases.

8. Playing Music Using Siri

To play music using Siri, press and hold the **Home** button or hold the phone up to your ear and wait for Siri to speak (Siri does not speak when activated on some models). Say one of the following phrases:

- Play Hotel California
- Play Coldplay shuffled
- Play Dave Matthews Band
- Play some folk
- Play my roadtrip playlist
- Shuffle my party playlist
- Play
- Pause
- Skip

Note: These phrases are only suggestions. Siri is flexible, and you can use many synonymous phrases.

9. Searching the Web and Asking Questions Using Siri

To search the web using Siri, press and hold the **Home** button or hold the phone up to your ear and wait for Siri to speak (Siri does not speak when activated on some models). Say one of the following phrases:

- Search the web for Apple News
- Search for chili recipes
- Google the humane society
- Search Wikipedia for Duckbilled Platypus
- Bing Secondhand Serenade
- How many calories in a doughnut?

- What is an 18% tip on $180.45 for six people?
- How long do cats live?
- What's 25 squared?
- How many dollars is 60 euros?
- How many days until Christmas?
- When is the next solar eclipse?
- Show me the Ursula Major constellation
- What is the meaning of life?
- What's the price of gasoline in Boston?

Note: These phrases are only suggestions. Siri is flexible, and you can use many synonymous phrases.

10. Looking Up Words in the Dictionary Using Siri

To look up words using Siri, press and hold the **Home** button or hold the phone up to your ear and wait for Siri to speak (Siri does not speak when activated on some models). Say one of the following phrases:

- What is the meaning of meticulous?
- Define albeit
- Look up the word jargon

Note: These phrases are only suggestions. Siri is flexible, and you can use many phrases synonymous with these suggestions.

11. Application-Specific Phrases for Siri

To search or set up reminders that relate to specific applications, press and hold the **Home** button or hold the iPhone up to your ear and wait for Siri to speak (Siri does not speak when activated on some models). Say one of the following phrases:

- Remind me about this when I get home (while viewing a web page)
- Show photos from Paris last June
- Remind me to reply to this (while viewing an email)
- Remind me to finish this note (while viewing a note in the Notes application)

Note: These phrases are only suggestions. Siri is flexible, and you can use many phrases synonymous with these suggestions.

Adjusting Wireless Settings

Table of Contents

1. Turning Airplane Mode On or Off
2. Turning Location Services On or Off
3. Customizing Cellular Data Usage (iPhone and iPad 4G only)
4. Turning Data Roaming On or Off (iPhone and iPad 4G only)
5. Setting Up a Virtual Private Network (VPN)
6. Turning Bluetooth On or Off
7. Using Wi-Fi to Sync Your Device with Your Computer

1. Turning Airplane Mode On or Off

Most airplanes do not allow wireless communications while in flight. Continue using the device by enabling Airplane mode before take-off. You may not place or receive calls, send or receive text messages or emails, or surf the Web while in Airplane mode. Airplane Mode is also useful when traveling outside of your area of service to avoid any roaming charges and to preserve battery life.

To turn Airplane Mode on or off, touch the ⚙ icon. The Settings screen appears, as shown

in **Figure 1**. Touch the ⬭ switch next to 'Airplane Mode'. The ⬤ switch appears and

Airplane mode is turned on. To turn off Airplane Mode, touch the ⬤ switch next to 'Airplane Mode'.

Figure 1: Settings Screen

2. Turning Location Services On or Off

Some applications, such as Maps, require the Location Services feature to be turned on, which determines your current location. To turn Location Services on or off:

1. Touch the [icon] icon. The Settings screen appears.
2. Scroll down and touch **Privacy**. The Privacy Settings screen appears, as shown in **Figure 2**.
3. Touch **Location Services**. The Location Services screen appears, as shown in **Figure 3**.
4. Touch the [switch] switch next to 'Location Services'. The [switch] switch appears and

    Location Services are turned on. To turn off Location Services, touch the [switch] switch next to 'Location Services'.

You can also customize the location preferences for each application listed on the Location Services screen. Touch the application, and then touch **Never** to turn off location services for that application permanently.

Scroll down and touch **System Services** to turn off Location Services for services, such as Find My iPad and HomeKit. You can even turn off the Frequent Locations feature, which tracks the locations that you visit most often to provide location-related information.

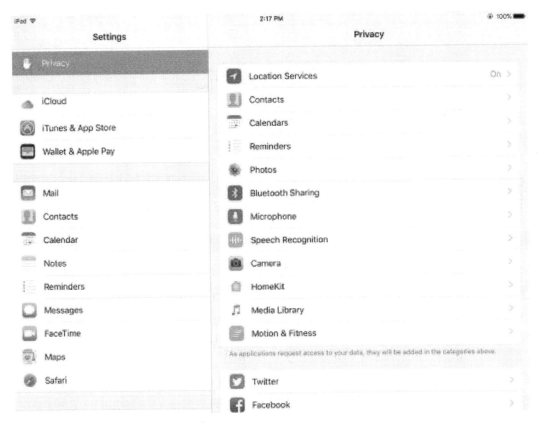

Figure 2: Privacy Settings Screen

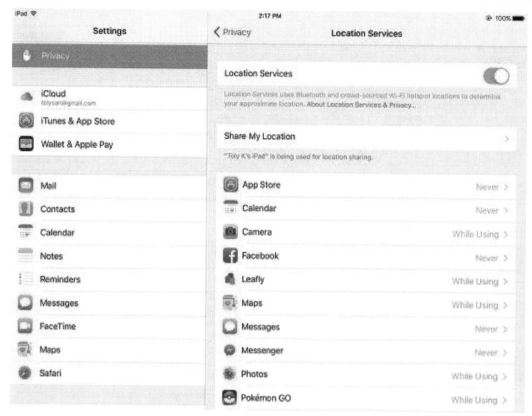

Figure 3: Location Services Screen

3. Customizing Cellular Data Usage (iPhone and iPad 4G only)

To surf the internet and download applications when not connected to Wi-Fi, you need to turn on cellular data. However, you can turn off cellular data if you wish to conserve battery life in an area with little or no 4G service. To turn cellular data on or off:

1. Touch the ⊚ icon. The Settings screen appears.
2. Touch **Cellular**. The Cellular Settings screen appears, as shown in **Figure 4**.

3. Touch the ⬭ switch next to 'Cellular Data'. The ⬤ switch appears and cellular data is turned on. To turn off Cellular Data, touch the ⬤ switch next to 'Cellular Data'.

You may also manage the cellular data usage from the Cellular Settings screen. To manage cellular data usage:

1. Touch the 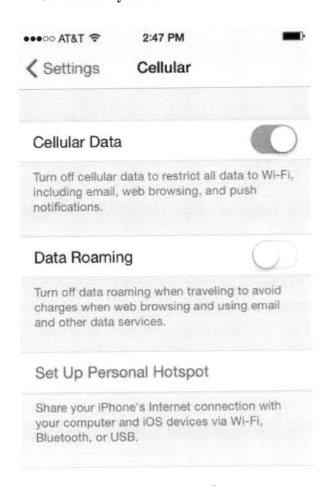 switch next to 'Mail', 'Passbook', or another application. Cellular data is turned off for the corresponding application.

2. Touch the switch next to the name of an application. Cellular data is turned on for the corresponding application.

3. Touch **System Services** to view the amount of data used by each service on your device.

Figure 4: Cellular Settings Screen

4. Turning Data Roaming On or Off (iPhone and iPad 4G only)

When you are in an area with no 4G coverage, the device can use the Data Roaming feature to acquire signal from other networks. Be aware that Data Roaming can be extremely costly. Contact your network provider for details. To turn Data Roaming on or off:

1. Touch the ⊚ icon. The Settings screen appears.
2. Touch **Cellular**. The Cellular Settings screen appears.
3. Touch the ⬭ switch next to 'Data Roaming'. The ⬬ switch appears and Data Roaming is turned on. To turn off Data Roaming, touch the ⬬ switch next to 'Data Roaming'.

5. Setting Up a Virtual Private Network (VPN)

You can use your device to connect to an external network, such as a corporate one. To set up a VPN:

1. Touch the ⊚ icon. The Settings screen appears.
2. Touch **General**. The General Settings screen appears, as shown in **Figure 5**.
3. Scroll down and touch **VPN**. The VPN screen appears, as shown in **Figure 6**.
4. Touch **Add VPN Configuration**. The Add VPN Configuration screen appears, as shown in **Figure 7**.
5. Touch each field and enter the required information.
6. Touch **Done**. The VPN is set up.

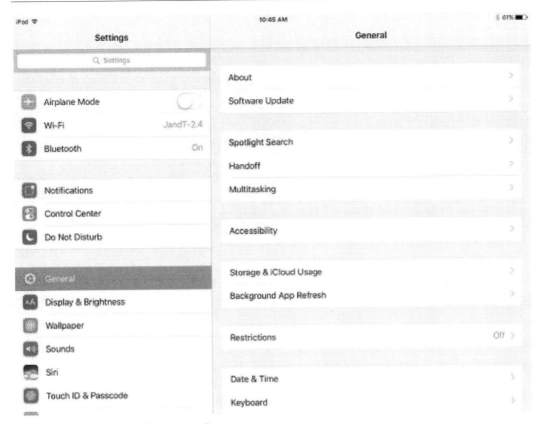

Figure 5: General Settings Screen

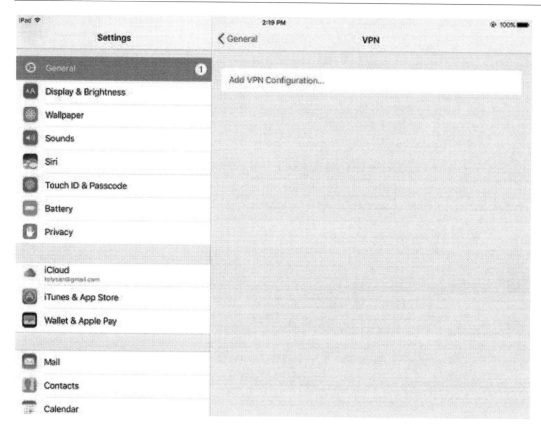

Figure 6: VPN Screen

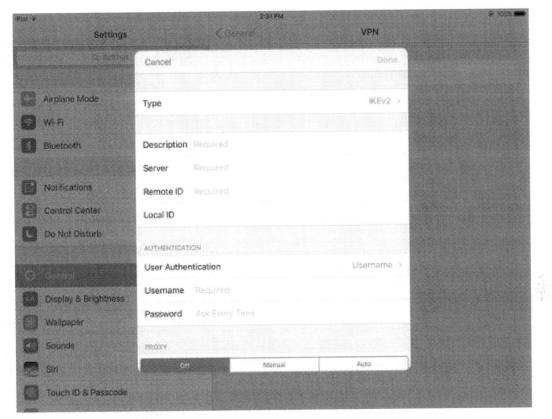

Figure 7: Add VPN Configuration Screen

6. Turning Bluetooth On or Off

A wireless Bluetooth headset or speaker can be used with the device. Be aware that leaving Bluetooth turned on while the headset or speaker is not in use may deplete battery life quickly. To turn Bluetooth on or off:

1. Touch the ⚙ icon. The Settings screen appears.
2. Touch **Bluetooth**. The Bluetooth Settings screen appears, as shown in **Figure 8**.

3. Touch the ⬤ switch next to 'Bluetooth'. Bluetooth is turned on and a list of devices appears. If there are no Bluetooth devices near the device, the list will be empty. To turn

   off Bluetooth, touch the ⬤ switch next to 'Bluetooth'. Bluetooth is turned off.

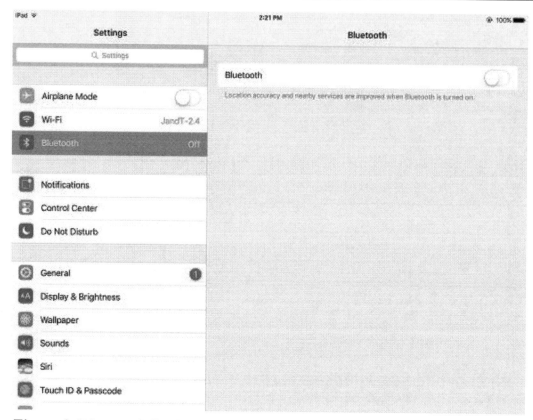

Figure 8: Bluetooth Settings Screen

7. Using Wi-Fi to Sync Your Device with Your Computer

Syncing your iOS 10 device with your computer allows you to save your media library on your computer in case you have to erase your device, or if you buy a new device. Instead of connecting your iOS 10 device to your computer to sync music, applications, and other media, you may sync wirelessly using Wi-Fi. Before you can use this feature, you must turn it on using iTunes on your computer. Refer to **https://www.apple.com/support/itunes/** if you need help using iTunes. To use Wi-Fi to sync your device with your computer:

Note: You may only use Wi-Fi syncing when your device is plugged in to an outlet, and Wi-Fi is turned on.

1. Connect your device to your computer using the cable that was provided when you purchased it. On some computers, iTunes opens automatically. If it does not, open iTunes.
2. Click the name of the device at the top or left side of the screen, depending on the version of iTunes. The device information screen appears, as shown in **Figure 9**, where an iPhone 4S is used as an example. You may need to first click **Continue**, and then click **Get Started** before this screen appears.
3. Click **Sync with this DEVICENAME over Wi-Fi**, where DEVICENAME can be either iPhone or iPad. A check mark appears next to 'Sync with this DEVICENAME'.
4. Click **Apply**. The Wi-Fi Sync feature is turned on.
5. Disconnect your device from your computer, and plug it into an outlet, as if you are charging it. Your device should automatically Sync with your computer. If it does not sync, follow steps 6-9 below.
6. Touch the ⚙ icon. The Settings screen appears.
7. Touch **General**. The General Settings screen appears.
8. Scroll down and touch **iTunes Wi-Fi Sync**. The iTunes Wi-Fi Sync screen appears.
9. Touch **Sync Now**. Your device syncs with your computer.

iPhone 4S

Julia's iPhone
`16GB` `█X█` 87%

Capacity: 12.79 GB
Phone Number:
Serial Number: C8PHWUSYDTD1

iOS 8.0

Your iPhone software is up to date. iTunes will automatically check for an update again on 9/13/2014.

[Check for Update] [Restore iPhone...]

Backups

Automatically Back Up

○ iCloud
  Back up the most important data on your iPhone to iCloud.

◉ This computer
  A full backup of your iPhone will be stored on this computer.

  ☐ Encrypt iPhone backup
    This will also back up account passwords used on this iPhone.

    [Change Password...]

Manually Back Up and Restore

Manually back up your iPhone to this computer or restore a backup stored on this computer.

[Back Up Now] [Restore Backup...]

Latest Backup:
Your iPhone has never been backed up to this computer.

Options

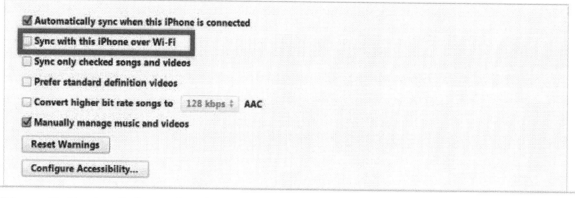

☑ **Automatically sync when this iPhone is connected**

☐ **Sync with this iPhone over Wi-Fi**

☐ **Sync only checked songs and videos**

☐ **Prefer standard definition videos**

☐ **Convert higher bit rate songs to** `128 kbps ⬍` **AAC**

☑ **Manually manage music and videos**

[Reset Warnings]

[Configure Accessibility...]

Figure 9: Device Information Screen (iPhone 4S)

Adjusting Sound Settings

Table of Contents

1. Turning Vibration On or Off (iPhone Only)
2. Turning Volume Button Functionality On or Off
3. Setting the Default Ringtone
4. Customizing Notification and Alert Sounds
5. Turning Lock Sounds On or Off
6. Turning Keyboard Clicks On or Off
7. Controlling Siri's Voice
8. Adjusting Siri Settings

1. Turning Vibration On or Off (iPhone Only)

The device can be set to vibrate every time it rings, or only while it is in Silent Mode. To turn Ringer Vibration on or off:

1. Touch the ⚙ icon. The Settings screen appears, as shown in **Figure 1**.
2. Scroll down and touch **Sounds**. The Sound Settings screen appears, as shown in **Figure 2**. This screenshot varies based on your device.
3. Touch the ⬭ switch next to 'Vibrate on Ring' under the 'Vibrate' section. The ⬭ switch appears and Ringer Vibration is turned on. The device will vibrate whenever there is an incoming call.
4. Touch the ⬭ switch. Ringer Vibration is turned off and the device will not vibrate for incoming calls.

To turn Silent Mode vibration on or off:

1. Touch the ⚙ icon. The Settings screen appears.
2. Touch **Sounds**. The Sound Settings screen appears.

3. Touch the ⬤ switch next to 'Vibrate on Silent' under the 'Vibrate' section.

The ⬤ switch appears and Silent Mode vibration is turned on. The device will vibrate whenever a call or message is received in Silent Mode.

4. Touch the ⬤ switch. Silent Mode Vibration is turned off. The device will not vibrate when it is in Silent Mode.

Note: To turn on Silent Mode on the device, put the vibration switch in the down position so that a red dot appears beneath the switch. Silent mode is turned on and the 🔕 icon appears on the screen. Refer to "Button Layout" on page 23 to view the location of the Vibration switch.

Figure 1: Settings Screen

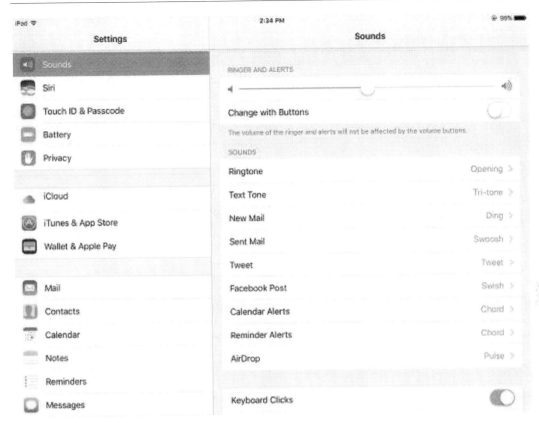

Figure 2: Sound Settings Screen

2. Turning Volume Button Functionality On or Off

The volume buttons can be used to adjust the volume of the media, alerts, and the ringer. When the volume button functionality is disabled, they no longer work. To turn the volume button functionality on or off:

1. Touch the ⚙ icon. The Settings screen appears.
2. Scroll down and touch **Sounds**. The Sound Settings screen appears.

3. Touch the ⬤ switch next to 'Change with Buttons' under the 'Ringer and Alerts' section. The ◯ switch appears and volume button functionality is turned off. To turn on Change with Buttons, touch the ◯ switch next to 'Change with Buttons'.

3. Setting the Default Ringtone

You may change the ringtone that sounds every time somebody calls you (FaceTime only on an iPad). To set a default ringtone:

1. Touch the 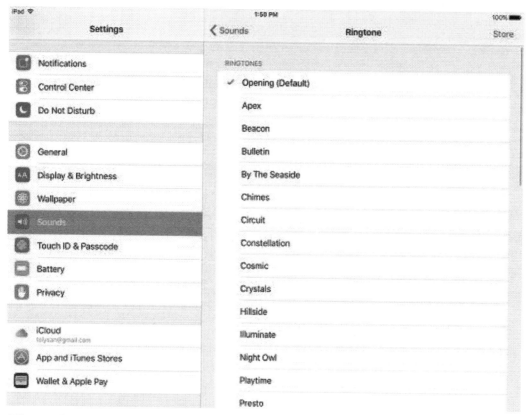 icon. The Settings screen appears.
2. Touch **Sounds**. The Sound Settings screen appears.
3. Touch **Ringtone**. A list of ringtones appears, as shown in **Figure 3**.
4. Touch a ringtone. The new default ringtone is selected and a preview plays.
5. Touch **Sounds** at the top of the screen. The new ringtone is set as the default.

*Note: You can also touch **Store** at the top of the screen to purchase more ringtones.*

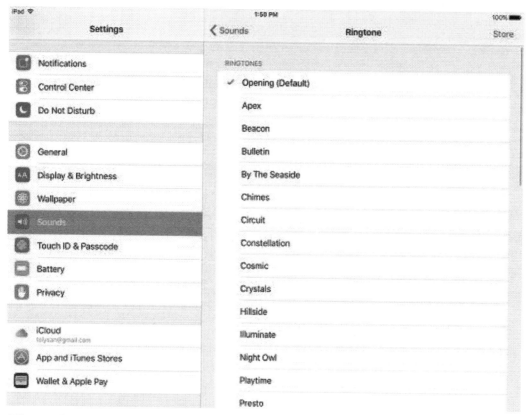

Figure 3: List of Ringtones

4. Customizing Notification and Alert Sounds

There are several notification and alert sounds that can be changed on the device. To customize notification and alert sounds:

1. Touch the ![icon] icon. The Settings screen appears.
2. Touch **Sounds**. The Sound Settings screen appears.
3. Touch one of the following options under the 'Sounds and Vibration Patterns' section to change the corresponding sound:

   - **Text Tone** - Plays when a new text message arrives.
   - **New Voicemail** - Plays when a new voicemail arrives (iPhone only).
   - **New Mail** - Plays when a new email arrives.
   - **Sent Mail** - Plays when an email is sent from the device.
   - **Tweet** - Plays when a new Tweet arrives.
   - **Facebook Post** - Plays when one of your Facebook friends creates a new post.
   - **Calendar Alerts** - Plays as a reminder for a calendar event.
   - **Reminder Alerts** - Plays as a notification of a previously set reminder.

5. Turning Lock Sounds On or Off

The device can make a sound every time it is locked or unlocked. By default, this sound is turned on. To turn Lock Sounds on or off:

1. Touch the ![icon] icon. The Settings screen appears.
2. Touch **Sounds**. The Sound Settings screen appears.
3. Scroll down and touch the ![switch] switch next to 'Lock Sound'. The ![switch] switch appears and lock sounds are turned off. To turn on lock sounds, touch the ![switch] switch next to 'Lock Sound'.

6. Turning Keyboard Clicks On or Off

The device can make a sound every time a key is touched on the virtual keyboard. By default, keyboard clicks are turned on. To turn Keyboard Clicks on or off:

1. Touch the ![icon] icon. The Settings screen appears.
2. Touch **Sounds**. The Sound Settings screen appears.

3. Touch the ![switch] switch next to 'Keyboard Clicks'. The ![switch] switch appears and Keyboard Clicks are turned off. To turn on Keyboard Clicks, touch the ![switch] switch next to 'Keyboard Clicks'.

7. Controlling Siri's Voice

By default, Siri's voice is never muted, even when you turn off your phone's volume. iOS 10 lets you turn Siri's voice on or off using the vibration switch. To turn on Siri Volume Control:

1. Touch the ![icon] icon. The Settings screen appears.
2. Touch **Siri**. The Siri Settings screen appears, as shown in **Figure 4**.
3. Touch **Voice Feedback**. The Voice Feedback screen appears, as shown in **Figure 5**.
4. Touch one of the following options to turn on the corresponding setting:

    *   **Control with Mute Setting** - Mute Siri using the Vibration switch.
    *   **Always On** - Leave Siri's voice feedback turned on permanently.
    *   **Hands-Free Only** - Only use Siri's voice feedback when Hey Siri is turned on, or when you connect a Bluetooth headset or headphones.

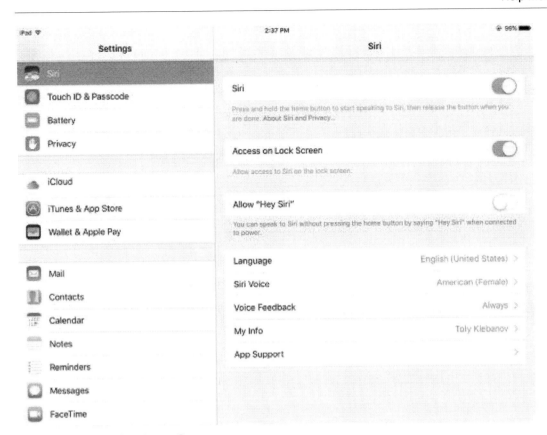

Figure 4: Siri Settings Screen

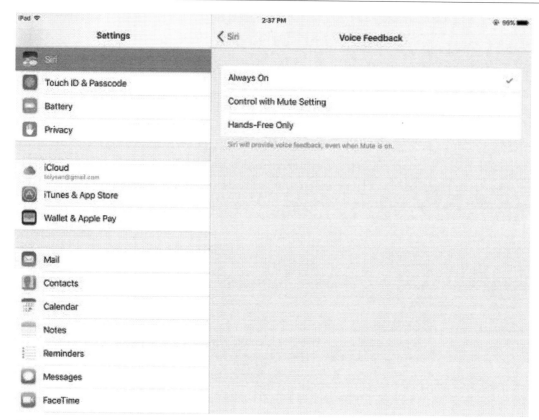

Figure 5: Voice Feedback Screen

8. Adjusting Siri Settings

You can adjust certain settings for Apple's voice assistant, Siri. To adjust the Siri settings:

1. Touch the ⬜ icon. The Settings screen appears.
2. Touch **Siri**. The Siri Settings screen appears.
3. Touch one of the following settings to change it:
   - **Access on Lock Screen** - Lets you use Siri while your device is locked.
   - **Allow "Hey Siri"** - Allows you to turn on Siri by saying "Hey Siri" without pressing and holding the Home button. Requires a short setup process.
   - **Language** - Select the language that Siri understands and uses to respond.
   - **Siri Voice** - Select the voice that Siri uses when responding.

Adjusting Language and Keyboard Settings

Table of Contents

1. Customizing Spelling and Grammar Settings
2. Adding an International Keyboard
3. Adding a Keyboard Shortcut
4. Changing the Operating System Language
5. Changing the Keyboard Layout
6. Changing the Region Format

1. Customizing Spelling and Grammar Settings

Customize the Spelling and Grammar settings on your device to improve typing accuracy when composing text messages or emails. To customize the Spelling and Grammar settings:

1. Touch the ⚙ icon. The Settings screen appears.
2. Touch **General**. The General Settings screen appears, as shown in **Figure 1**.
3. Scroll down and touch **Keyboard**. The Keyboard Settings screen appears, as shown in **Figure 2**.
4. Touch one of the switches on the right side of the screen to turn the corresponding setting on or off:
   - **Auto-Capitalization** - Capitalizes the first word of every sentence automatically.
   - **Auto-Correction** - Suggests and makes spelling corrections while you type.
   - **Check Spelling** - Underlines all misspelled words.
   - **Enable Caps Lock** - Allows you to turn Caps Lock on by quickly touching

     the ⇧ key twice on the virtual keyboard. While Caps Lock is turned on, all

     capital letters are typed without the need to use the ⇧ key.
   - **Predictive** - The Predictive Text feature offers suggestions for the next word in a sentence as you type, which is intelligently based on the words that you have already typed.
   - **Split Keyboard** - Allows you to use a split keyboard, which is useful when holding the iPad horizontally, and typing using your thumbs. To activate the split keyboard, touch one of the bottom corners of the keyboard, and slide your finger up.

- **."" Shortcut** - Allows a period and an extra space to be inserted when you quickly touch the space bar twice.

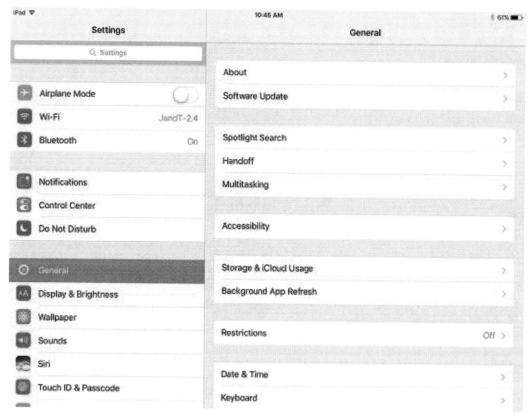

Figure 1: General Settings Screen

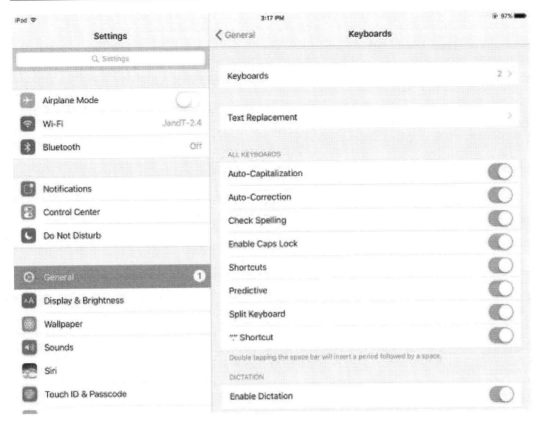

Figure 2: Keyboard Settings Screen

2. Adding an International Keyboard

The device allows you to use international keyboards when entering text on the virtual keyboard. To add an international keyboard:

1. Touch the ![icon] icon. The Settings screen appears.
2. Touch **General**. The General Settings screen appears.
3. Scroll down and touch **Keyboard**. The Keyboard Settings screen appears.
4. Touch **Keyboards**. The Keyboards screen appears, as shown in **Figure 3**.
5. Touch **Add New Keyboard**. A list of international keyboards appears, as shown in **Figure 4**.
6. Touch a keyboard. The keyboard is added. While typing, touch the ![globe] key at the bottom of the virtual keyboard to switch to an international one.
7. You may remove a keyboard from the list by touching and holding it, and then sliding your finger to the left until 'Delete' appears. Touch **Delete** to remove the keyboard.

Note: If you only add the Emoji keyboard (emoticons) in addition to the English keyboard, the key appears instead of the 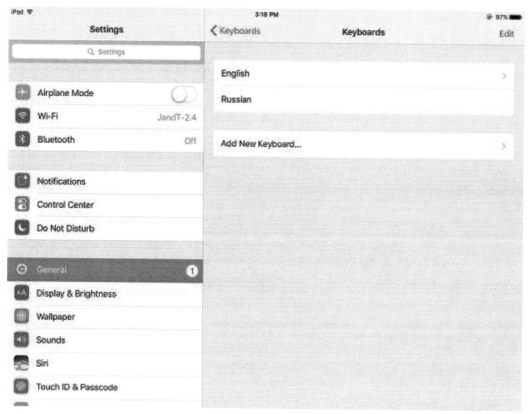 key.

Figure 3: Keyboards Screen

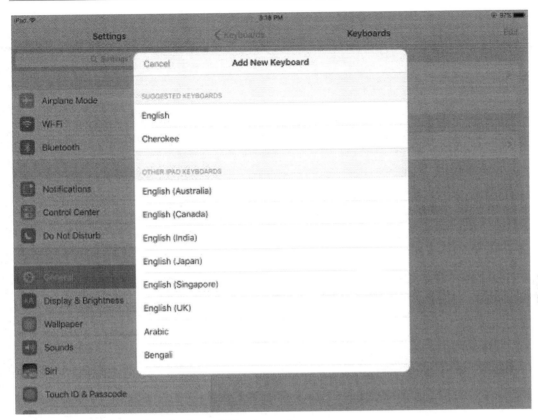

Figure 4: List of International Keyboards

3. Adding a Keyboard Shortcut

The device allows you to add custom Keyboard shortcuts. For example, "ur" for "your" or "ttyl" for "talk to you later" are substituted when the corresponding abbreviation is typed. To add a Keyboard shortcut:

1. Touch the ⚙ icon. The Settings screen appears.
2. Touch **General**. The General Settings screen appears.
3. Scroll down and touch **Keyboard**. The Keyboard Settings screen appears.
4. Touch **Text Replacement**. A list of existing shortcuts appears, as shown in **Figure 5**.
5. Touch the ✛ icon. The Add Text Replacement screen appears, as shown in **Figure 6**.
6. Enter the desired phrase to be substituted for the shortcut. Touch **return**.
7. Enter the desired shortcut and touch **Save** at the top of the screen. The keyboard shortcut is added. To use the shortcut, type it and touch the space bar.

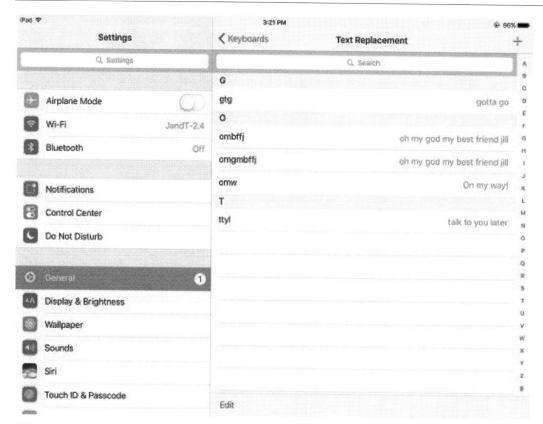

Figure 5: List of Existing Shortcuts

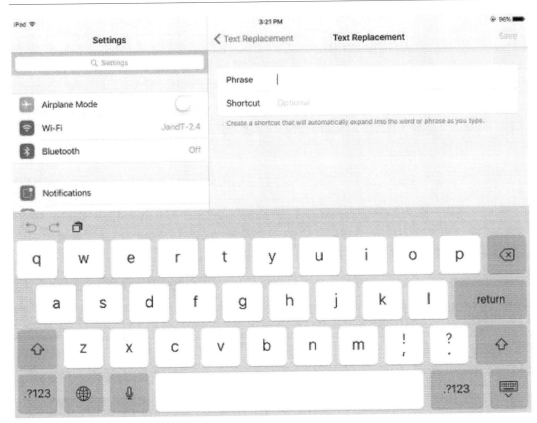

Figure 6: Text Replacement Screen

4. Changing the Operating System Language

The iOS on the device can be changed to display all menus and options in a language other than English. To change the Operating System Language:

1. Touch the 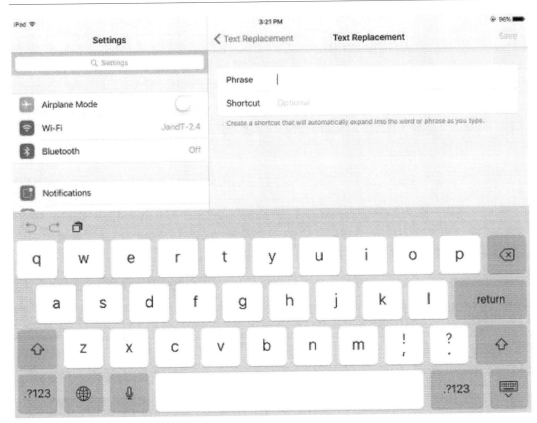 icon. The Settings screen appears.
2. Touch **General**. The General Settings screen appears.
3. Scroll down and touch **Language & Region**. The Language & Region screen appears, as shown in **Figure 7**.
4. Touch **iPhone Language** or **iPad Language**, depending on the type of your device. A list of available languages appears, as shown in **Figure 8**.
5. Touch a language, and then touch **Done** at the top of the screen. A confirmation dialog appears.
6. Touch **Continue**. The selected language is applied and all menus and the options reflect the change.

Note: It may take some time to install the language. This delay is normal.

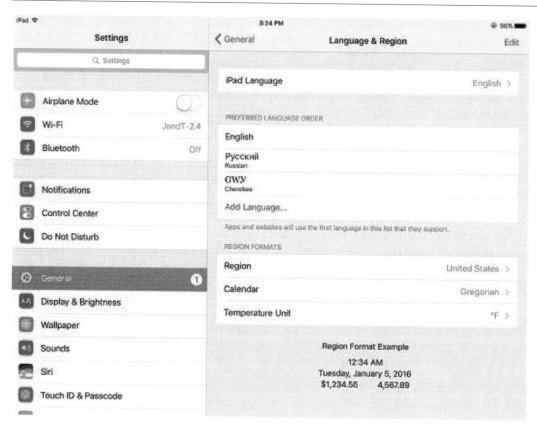

Figure 7: Language & Region Screen

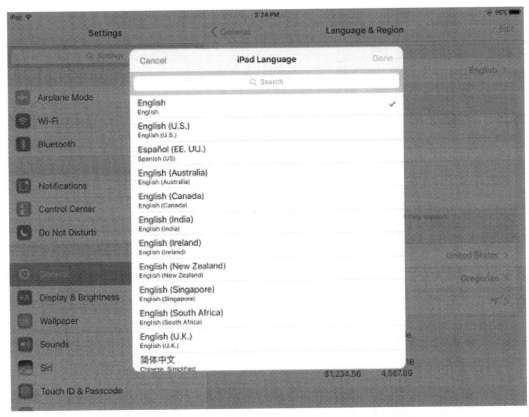

Figure 8: List of Available Languages

5. Changing the Keyboard Layout

The layout of the keyboard in most languages can be changed, according to personal preference. For instance, the English keyboard can be set display in default QWERTY, as shown in **Figure 9**, AZERTY, as shown in **Figure 10**, or QWERTZ as shown in **Figure 11**. To change the Keyboard Layout:

1. Touch the ⚙ icon. The Settings screen appears.
2. Touch **General**. The General Settings screen appears.
3. Scroll down and touch **Keyboard**. The Keyboard Settings screen appears.
4. Touch **Keyboards**. The Keyboards screen appears.
5. Touch the language of the keyboard that you wish to change. The Keyboard Layout screen appears.
6. Touch the desired layout. The new Keyboard Layout is set.

Note: The English keyboard layouts are shown below only as an example. The keyboard layouts vary based on the language that you select.

Figure 9: QWERTY Keyboard

Figure 10: AZERTY Keyboard

Figure 11: QWERTZ Keyboard

6. Changing the Region Format

The region format on the device determines how dates, times, and phone numbers are universally displayed. For instance, a European country may display the 30th day of the first month in the year 2011 as 30/01/2011, whereas the U.S. would display the same date as 01/30/2011. To change the region format:

1. Touch the 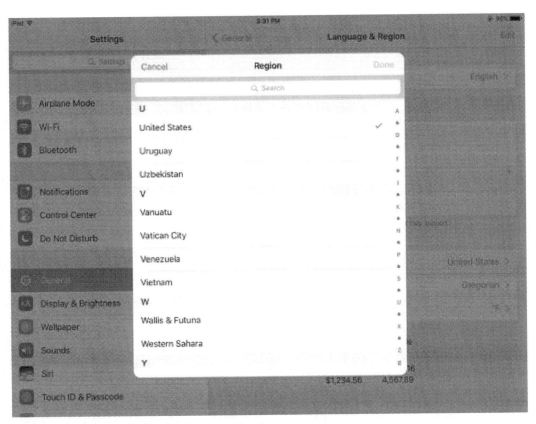 icon. The Settings screen appears.
2. Touch **General**. The General Settings screen appears.
3. Touch **Language & Region**. The Language & Region screen appears.
4. Touch **Region**. A list of regions appears, as shown in **Figure 12**.
5. Touch the desired region. The new region format is set.

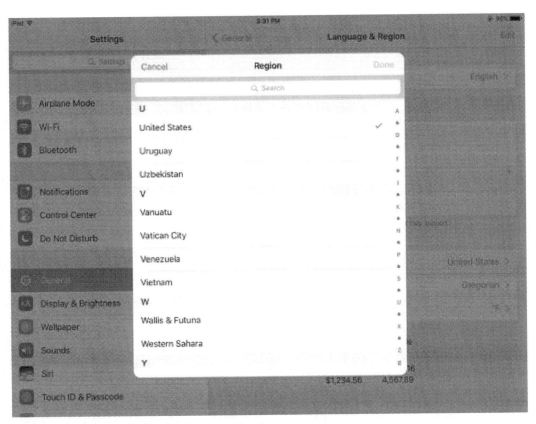

Figure 12: List of Regions

Adjusting General Settings

Table of Contents

1. Changing Auto-Lock Settings
2. Adjusting the Brightness
3. Turning Night Shift On or Off
4. Assigning a Passcode Lock or Fingerprint Lock
5. Turning 24-Hour Mode On or Off
6. Resetting the Home Screen Layout
7. Resetting All Settings
8. Erasing and Restoring the Device
9. Managing Notification Settings
10. Changing the Wallpaper
11. Restricting Access to Private Information
12. Turning Raise to Wake On or Off (iPhone 6S and Later Only)

1. Changing Auto-Lock Settings

The device can lock itself when it is idle in order to save battery life, and to avoid unintentionally pressing buttons. When it is locked, the device can still receive calls and text messages. By default, the device is set to automatically lock after one minute. To change the length of time that will pass before the device locks itself:

1. Touch the ⊚ icon. The Settings screen appears.
2. Touch **Display & Brightness**. The Display & Brightness screen appears, as shown in **Figure 1**.
3. Touch **Auto-Lock**. The Auto-Lock screen appears, as shown in **Figure 2**.
4. Touch an amount of time, or touch **Never** if you do not want the device to automatically lock itself. The change is applied and the device will wait the selected amount of time before automatically locking itself.

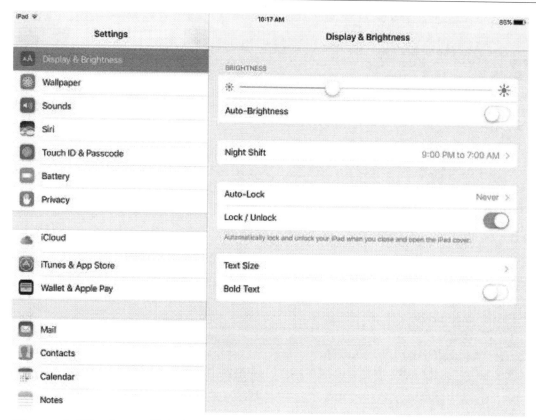

Figure 1: Display & Brightness Screen

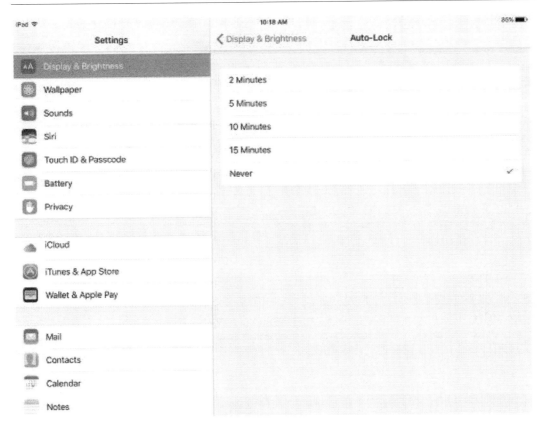

Figure 2: Auto-Lock Screen

2. Adjusting the Brightness

You may wish to increase the brightness of the screen on your device when you are in a sunny area. On the other hand, you may wish to decrease the brightness in a dark area to conserve battery life. You can also turn Auto-Brightness on or off, which will determine whether or not the device automatically sets the brightness based on the lighting conditions. To adjust the brightness:

1. Touch the ⊙ icon. The Settings screen appears.
2. Touch **Display & Brightness**. The Display & Brightness Settings screen appears.
3. Touch the ⊙ on the ▬▬▬▬○ bar and drag it towards the small ☀ icon to decrease the brightness or towards the large ☀ icon to increase it.
4. Touch the ⬤ switch next to 'Auto-Brightness' to disable Auto-Brightness, or touch the ○ switch to enable it. Auto-Brightness it disabled or enabled.

Note: While Auto-Brightness is enabled, you can still temporarily adjust the brightness of the screen. However, as soon as the lighting conditions change, the device will automatically change the brightness.

3. Turning Night Shift On or Off

The Night Shift feature allows you to set the display to use warm colors, which are easier on the eyes. This is a feature that is especially useful in the evening hours when you do not want to strain your eyes. In addition to turning Night Shift on or off, you can schedule it to automatically turn on during a certain time period. To configure Night Shift:

1. Touch the [icon] icon. The Settings screen appears.
2. Touch **Display & Brightness**. The Display & Brightness Settings screen appears.
3. Touch **Night Shift**. The Night Shift screen appears, as shown in **Figure 3**.
4. Touch **Manually Enable Until Tomorrow**. Night Shift is turned on until 12:00am on the following day. To schedule Night Shift, touch **From To** and select a time range.

You can also manually turn on Night Shift in the Control Center by touching **Night Shift**. Refer to *"Accessing Quick Settings through the Control Center"* on page 44 to learn more.

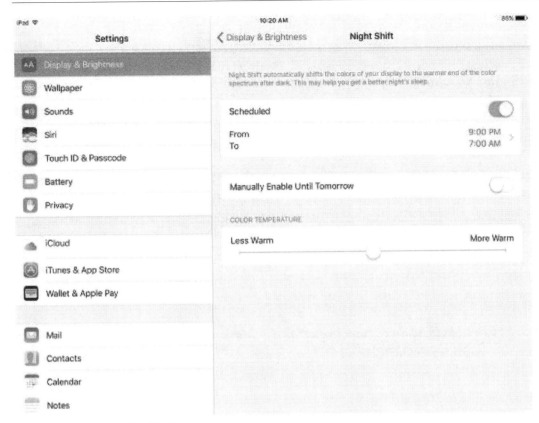

Figure 3: Night Shift Screen

4. Assigning a Passcode Lock or Fingerprint Lock

The device can prompt for a four-digit or alphanumeric password, or your fingerprint before unlocking. This feature is only compatible with the following devices:

- iPhone 5S or later
- iPad Pro
- iPad Air 2 or later
- iPad Mini 3 or later

To set up a password lock:

1. Touch the ⚙ icon. The Settings screen appears.
2. Touch **Touch ID & Passcode**. The Touch ID & Passcode screen appears, as shown in **Figure 4**.

3. Touch **Turn Passcode On**. The Set Passcode screen appears, as shown in **Figure 5**. To set a 4-Digit numeric, an alphanumeric, or a custom numeric passcode, touch **Passcode Options**, and select an option from the Passcode Options list, as shown in **Figure 6**.
4. Enter a passcode. A confirmation screen appears.
5. Enter the passcode again. The new passcode is set.
6. Touch one of the following options on the Passcode Lock screen to change the corresponding setting:

   • **Require Passcode** - Set the time the device waits before asking the user for the passcode. It is recommended to choose the default, **Immediately**, since an unauthorized user will not have access to your device for any period of time if this option is chosen. Choosing one of the other options causes the device to wait a set amount of time after being locked before requiring a passcode.
   • **Erase Data** - Erases all data after a user enters the passcode incorrectly ten times in a row.

Warning: You will not be able to recover your data if this feature is on when an incorrect passcode is entered ten times consecutively.

Set Fingerprint Lock

To set up a fingerprint lock:

1. Set up a password lock. Refer to the instructions **above** to learn how.
2. Touch **Add a fingerprint**. The Fingerprint Setup screen appears.
3. Lift and rest your finger on the Home button repeatedly. Keep doing this until the Fingerprint Confirmation screen appears, as shown in **Figure 7**. Your fingerprint can now be used to unlock the device. To unlock the device, activate the screen by pressing the Home or Sleep/Wake button, and scan your fingerprint.

Note: You must use the same thumb that you scanned in step 3 to unlock your device every time.

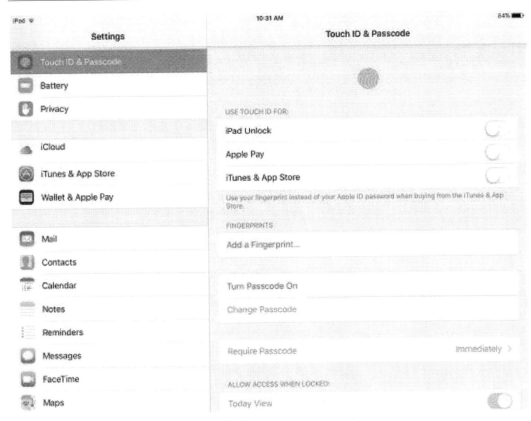

Figure 4: Touch ID & Passcode Screen

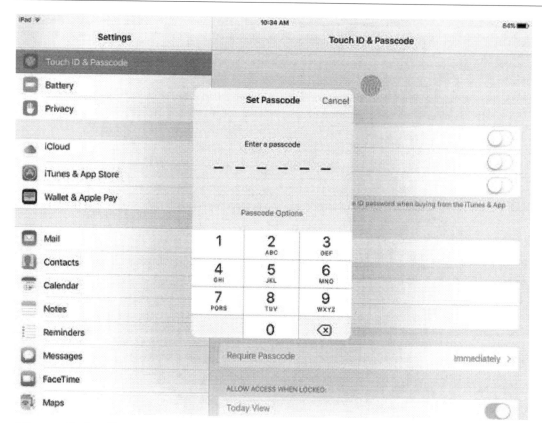

Figure 5: Set Passcode Screen

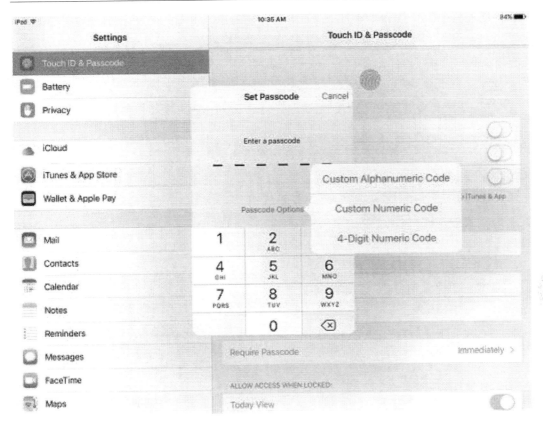

Figure 6: Passcode Options

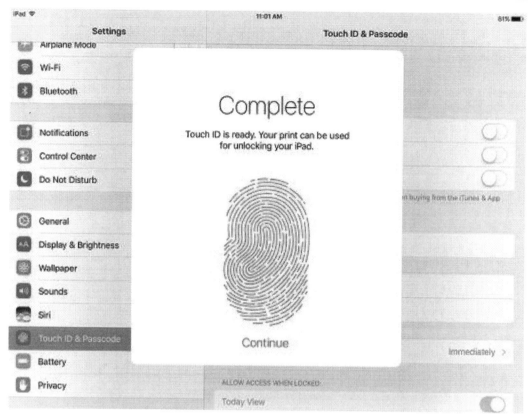

Figure 7: Fingerprint Confirmation Screen

5. Turning 24-Hour Mode On or Off

The device can display the time in regular 12-hour mode or in 24-hour mode, commonly referred to as military time. To turn 24-hour mode on or off:

1. Touch the ⊚ icon. The Settings screen appears.
2. Touch **General**. The General Settings screen appears.
3. Scroll down and touch **Date & Time**. The Date & Time screen appears, as shown in **Figure 8**.

4. Touch the ⊙ switch next to '24-Hour Time'. The ⬤ switch appears 24-Hour mode is turned on. To turn off 24-Hour mode, touch the ⬤ switch next to '24-Hour Time'.

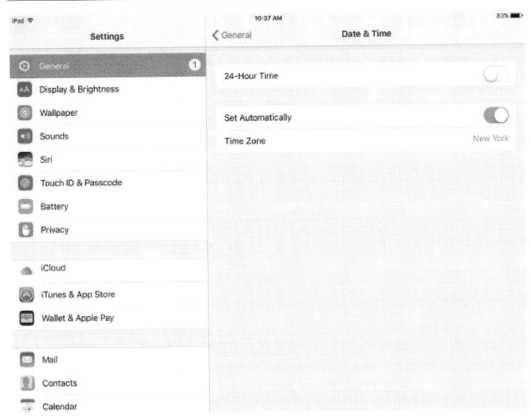

Figure 8: Date & Time Screen

6. Resetting the Home Screen Layout

You can reset the Home screen on your device to look like it did when you first purchased it. To reset the Home Screen Layout:

Note: Resetting the Home screen layout does not delete any applications, but simply rearranges them on the Home screen.

1. Touch the 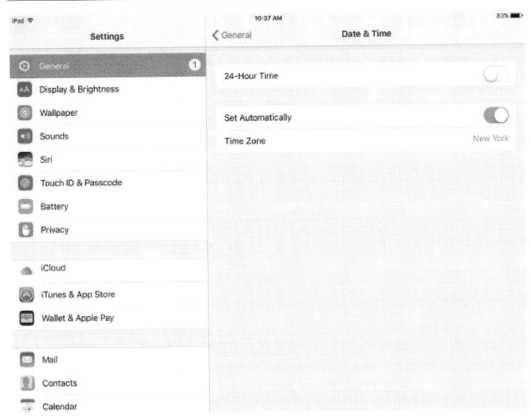 icon. The Settings screen appears.
2. Touch **General**. The General Settings screen appears.
3. Scroll down and touch **Reset**. The Reset screen appears, as shown in **Figure 9**.
4. Touch **Reset Home Screen Layout**. A confirmation dialog appears at the bottom of the screen.
5. Touch **Reset Home Screen**. The Home Screen Layout is reset.

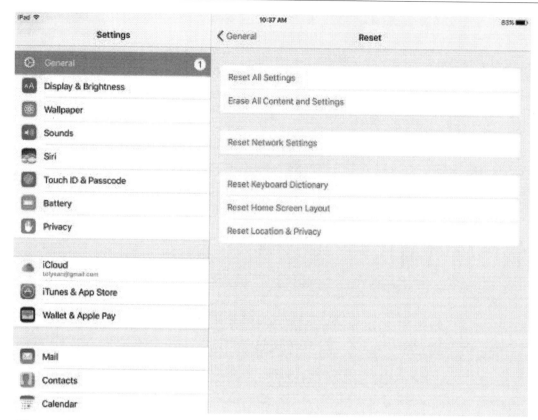

Figure 9: Reset Screen

7. Resetting All Settings

You can reset all of the settings on your device to the state they were in when you first purchased it. To reset all settings:

Note: Resetting the settings will NOT delete any data from your device.

1. Touch the ⊚ icon. The Settings screen appears.
2. Touch **General**. The General Settings screen appears.
3. Scroll down and touch **Reset**. The Reset screen appears.
4. Touch **Reset All Settings**. A confirmation dialog appears at the bottom of the screen. You will also need to enter your passcode, if you have one.
5. Touch **Reset All Settings**. All settings are reset to defaults.

8. Erasing and Restoring the Device

You can delete all of the data and reset all settings to completely restore the device to its original condition. To erase and restore the device to its original condition:

Warning: Any erased data is not recoverable. Make sure that you back up all of the data that you wish to keep.

1. Touch the ⚙ icon. The Settings screen appears.
2. Touch **General**. The General Settings screen appears.
3. Touch **Reset**. The Reset screen appears.
4. Touch **Erase All Content and Settings**. Enter the device's passcode if you have set one. A confirmation dialog appears.
5. Touch **Erase**. The device is erased and restored to its original condition.

9. Managing Notification Settings

You may customize the types of notifications that appear in the Notifications Center. To manage notification settings:

1. Touch the ⚙ icon. The Settings screen appears.
2. Touch **Notifications**. The Notifications Settings appear, as shown in **Figure 10**.
3. Touch one of the notification types, such as device or Messages, to turn the notifications on or off, or to customize the number of notifications that appear. The Notification Customization screen appears, as shown in **Figure 11** (Messages Notification Customization).
4. Touch the ⬤ switch next to 'Allow Notifications'. The ⬤ switch appears and notifications will no longer appear for the selected type.
5. Touch one of the following options to customize the notifications:

Note: The following options vary based on the notification type. You may also need to first touch your account, as in the case of adjusting Mail notifications.

- **Show in Notification Center** - Select the number of recent items that should appear in the Notifications Center for the selected type.
- **Sounds** - Select the sound that plays when a new notification of the selected type arrives.

- **Badge App Icon** - Turn the notification type icon that appears next to a notification on or off.
- **Show on Lock Screen** - Allow notifications of the selected type to appear on the Lock screen.
- **Alert Style When Unlocked** - Touch **None**, **Banners**, or **Alerts** to select the way in which notifications appear for the selected type.

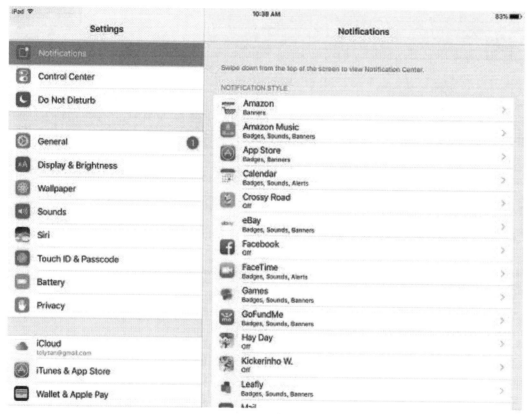

Figure 10: Notifications Settings

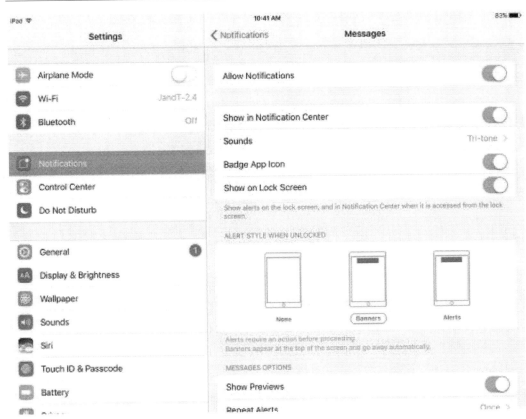

Figure 11: Notification Customization Screen

10. Changing the Wallpaper

The wallpaper is the image that appears on the Lock screen, and on the Home screen behind the application icons. To change the wallpaper:

1. Touch the ⚙ icon. The Settings screen appears.
2. Touch **Wallpaper**. The Wallpaper Settings appear, as shown in **Figure 12**.
3. Touch **Choose a New Wallpaper**. The Wallpaper Selection screen appears, as shown in **Figure 13**.
4. Touch the image above 'Dynamic' or 'Stills', or touch one of the photo albums under 'Photos'. The corresponding image thumbnails appear.
5. Touch an image thumbnail. The image appears in full-screen, as shown in **Figure 14**.
6. Touch **Set Lock Screen**, **Set Home Screen**, or **Set Both** to set the corresponding wallpaper. The new wallpaper is set.

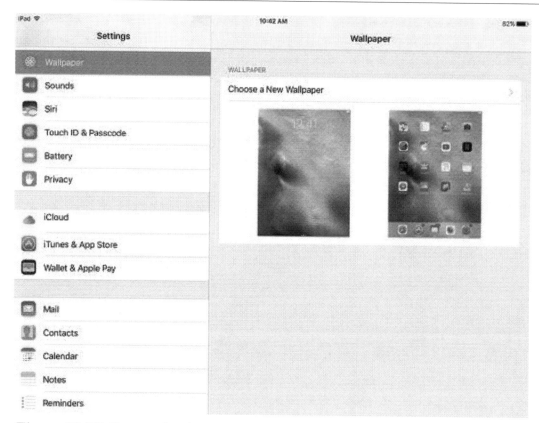

Figure 12: Wallpaper Settings

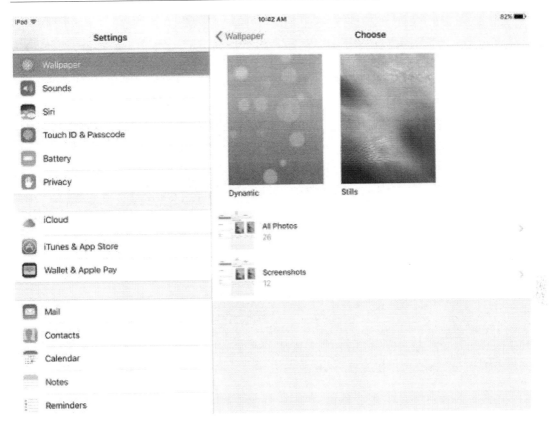

Figure 13: Wallpaper Selection

Figure 14: Wallpaper Image in Full-Screen

11. Restricting Access to Private Information

Some applications may request to use your some of the information stored on your device, or even to access your camera. If you touch **Allow**, the application will have access to the requested information until you take away the access. To restrict access to private information:

1. Touch the ⬡ icon. The Settings screen appears.
2. Touch **Privacy**. The Privacy Settings screen appears, as shown in **Figure 15**.
3. Touch one of the information types, such as 'Contacts' or 'Calendars'. The list of applications appear that have requested access to the selected type of information, as shown in **Figure 16** (Microphone).

4. Touch the ⬤ switch next to the name of the requesting application. The ◯ switch appears, and the selected application will no longer have access to the type of information selected in step 3.

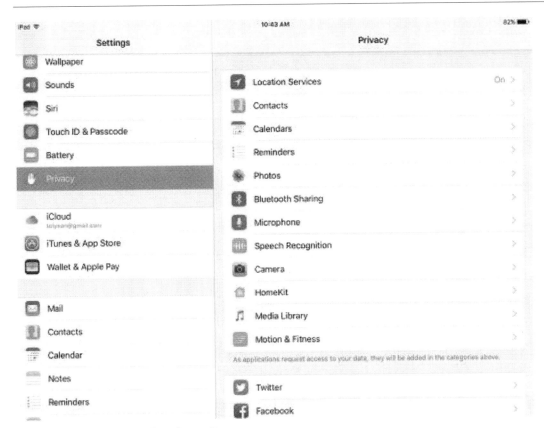

Figure 15: Privacy Settings Screen

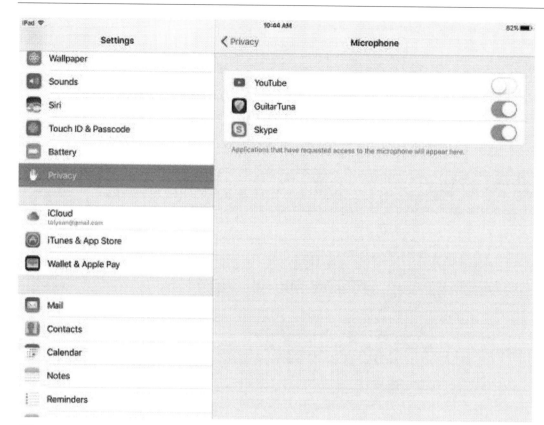

Figure 16: List of Applications that Have Requested Access

12. Turning Raise to Wake On or Off (iPhone 6S and Later Only)

The Raise to Wake feature allows you to turn on your iPhone's screen when you pick it up or take it out of your pocket. Then, all you have to do is unlock it. To turn Raise to Wake on or off:

1. Touch the [icon] icon. The Settings screen appears.
2. Touch **Display & Brightness**. The Display & Brightness Settings screen appears.
3. Touch the [switch] switch next to 'Raise to Wake'. The Raise to Wake feature is turned on.

   To turn off Raise to Wake, touch the [switch] switch next to 'Raise to Wake'.

Adjusting Accessibility Settings

Table of Contents

1. Managing Vision Accessibility Features
2. Managing Hearing Accessibility Features
3. Turning Guided Access On or Off
4. Managing Physical & Motor Accessibility Features

1. Managing Vision Accessibility Features

Vision accessibility features allow people with visual disabilities to use the device with greater ease. To manage vision accessibility features:

1. Touch the [icon] icon. The Settings screen appears.
2. Touch **General**. The General Settings screen appears, as shown in **Figure 1**.
3. Touch **Accessibility**. The Accessibility Settings screen appears, as shown in **Figure 2**.
4. Touch one of the following options to turn vision accessibility features on or off:
   - **VoiceOver** - This feature speaks an item on the screen when you touch it once, activates it when you touch it twice, and scrolls through a list or page of text when you touch the screen with three fingers. You can use a variety of voices for Voiceover, including Siri's male or female voice.
   - **Zoom** - This features zooms in on an item when you touch the screen twice using three fingers, moves around when you drag three fingers on the screen, and changes the level of zoom when you touch the screen with three fingers twice and drag.
   - **Magnifier** - This feature lets you use the device's camera as a magnifying glass. When enabled, press the Home button three times quickly to turn it on.
   - **Invert Colors** (Under **Display Accommodations**) - This feature inverts all of the colors on the screen. For instance, black text on a white screen becomes white text on a black screen.
   - **Color Filters** (Under **Display Accommodations**) - This feature changes all color on the device's screen to black and white, red/green, green/red ,or blue/yellow, depending on the type of color blindness.
   - **Larger Text** - This feature increases the default size of the font. Use the font slider to adjust the default font size.

- **Bold Text** - This feature makes all text on the device bold in order to make it easier to read. Enabling or disabling this feature requires you to restart the device.
- **Button Shapes** - This feature allows all buttons, such as the back button in the upper left-hand corner of each menu screen, to have outlines.
    - **Increase Contrast** - This feature improves the contrast on certain backgrounds in order to make it easier to read certain text.
    - **Reduce Motion** - This feature turns off all screen animations, such as when you close an application to return to the Home screen.
    - **On/Off Labels** - This feature turns ⬭ and ⬮ switches into ⬭ and ⬮ switches, respectively.

Speech:

- **Speak Selection** (Under **Speech**) - This feature allows all text on the screen to be spoken aloud when you select it and touch **Speak**.
- **Speak Screen** (Under **Speech**) - This feature allows all the contents of the screen to be described when you touch the top of the screen with two fingers and slide down.
- **Speak Auto-text** (Under **Speech**) - This feature speaks every auto-correction or auto-capitalization as you enter text in any text field, including text messages and emails.

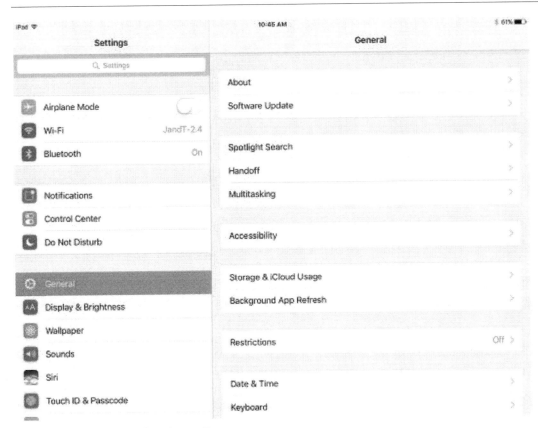

Figure 1: General Settings Screen

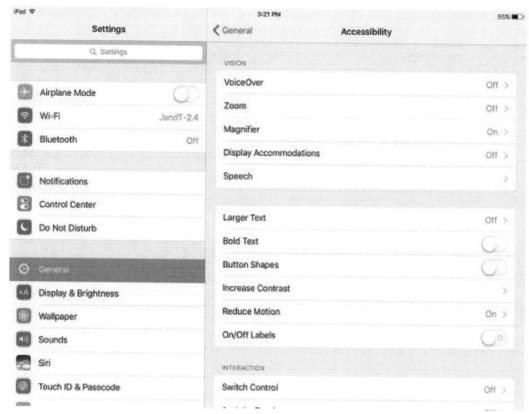

Figure 2: Accessibility Settings Screen

2. Managing Hearing Accessibility Features

Hearing accessibility features allow people with hearing disabilities to use the device with greater ease. To manage hearing accessibility features:

1. Touch the ⊚ icon. The Settings screen appears.
2. Touch **General**. The General Settings screen appears.
3. Touch **Accessibility**. The Accessibility Settings screen appears.
4. Touch one of the following options to turn hearing accessibility features on or off:

    - **Subtitles & Captioning** - This feature allows subtitles and closed captioning to be enabled for videos, where available.

    - **Audio Descriptions** - This feature allows automatically plays audio descriptions for certain media, where available.

    - **LED Flash for Alerts (iPhone only)** - This feature allows the camera flash to be used to provide notification alerts, such as incoming calls or text messages.

    - **Mono Audio** - This feature turns off stereo audio, leaving only one speaker working.

3. Turning Guided Access On or Off

Guided Access is a feature that is made for people with learning disabilities, allowing the user to stay in a single application and control the features that are available. To turn Guided Access on or off:

1. Touch the ⊚ icon. The Settings screen appears.
2. Touch **General**. The General Settings screen appears.
3. Touch **Accessibility**. The Accessibility Settings screen appears.
4. Scroll down and touch **Guided Access**. The Guided Access Settings screen appears, as shown in **Figure 3**.
5. Touch the ⬭ switch next to 'Guided Access'. Guided Access is turned on.
6. Touch **Passcode Settings**, then Set Guided Access Passcode to set up a passcode that will allow you to exit the application when you are done using it.

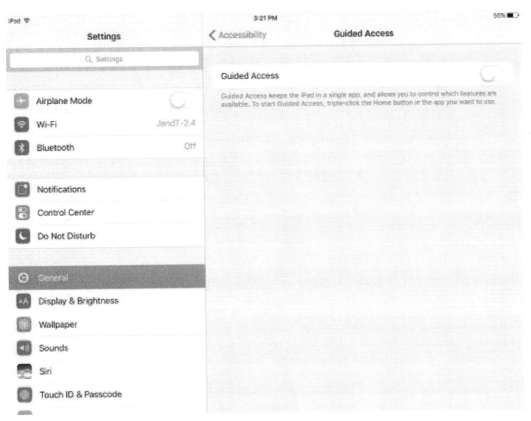

Figure 3: Guided Access Settings Screen

4. Managing Physical & Motor Accessibility Features

Physical and Motor accessibility features allow people with motor disabilities to use the device with greater ease. To manage physical & motor accessibility features:

1. Touch the ⚙ icon. The Settings screen appears.
2. Touch **General**. The General Settings screen appears.
3. Touch **Accessibility**. The Accessibility Settings screen appears.
4. Touch one of the following options to turn physical and motor accessibility features on or off:

    - **Switch Control** - This feature allows an adaptive accessory to be used to highlight items on the screen to control the functions of the device. The Switch Control screen allows various settings, such as timing, switch stabilization, point scanning, audio, and visual settings, to be adjusted.

    - **Assistive Touch** - This feature allows you to create custom gestures in order to access various services on the device.

    - **Home Button** - This feature allows you to slow down the speed at which you need to press the Home button to access certain features.

    - **Call Audio Routing** - This feature allows you to answer calls directly on your headset or speakerphone by default.

    - **Shake to Undo** - This feature allows you to turn the Shake to Undo feature on or off. By default, shaking the device causes it ask you whether you would like to undo typing. Refer to **Quickly Deleting Recently Typed Text** to learn more.

    - **Accessibility Shortcut** - This feature allows you to select an accessibility feature that will be turned on when you press the Home button three times quickly at any time. If you choose more than one feature, a menu will appear allowing you to select the Accessibility feature that you wish to enable.

Touch Accommodations

This feature allows you to customize certain touch gestures when interacting with the device's screen. The following settings are turned on or off when this setting is enabled or disabled.

- **Hold Duration** - Adjust the amount of time that you must touch and hold the screen before a touch is recognized.
- **Ignore Repeat** - Adjust the amount of time that passes before a touch is recognized as a separate touch from the first. For instance, if you set the time to 2 seconds and touch the screen twice within one second, only the first touch is recognized.
- **Tap Assistance** - Allows you to touch the screen and drag your finger to make a selection. Your touch is not recognized until you lift your finger. Touch **Use Initial Touch Location** to have the device register your touch where you first touched the screen. Touch **Use Final Touch Location** to have the device register your touch where you last touched the screen.

Adjusting Phone Settings (iPhone Only)

Table of Contents

1. Turning Call Forwarding On or Off
2. Turning Call Waiting On or Off
3. Turning Caller ID On or Off
4. Turning the International Assist On or Off
5. Blocking Specific Numbers
6. Editing Preset Text Message Responses

1. Turning Call Forwarding On or Off

The device can be set to forward all calls to a specified number. To turn Call Forwarding on or off:

1. Touch the ⚙ icon. The Settings screen appears, as shown in **Figure 1**.
2. Scroll down and touch **Phone**. The Phone Settings screen appears, as shown in **Figure 2**.
3. Touch **Call Forwarding**. The Call Forwarding screen appears.
4. Touch the ⬭ switch next to 'Call Forwarding'. The 'Forward to' field appears, as shown in **Figure 3**.
5. Use the keypad to enter the phone number to which the phone should forward. When finished, touch **Call Forwarding** at the top of the screen. Call Forwarding is set up, and the Call Forwarding screen appears.

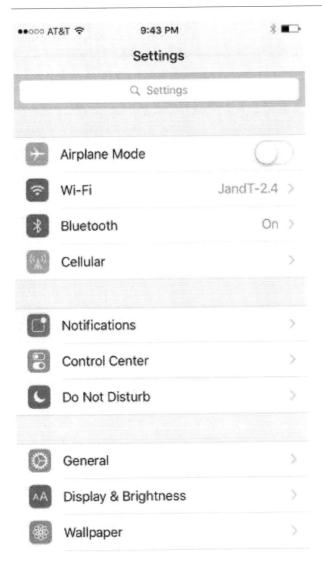

Figure 1: Settings Screen

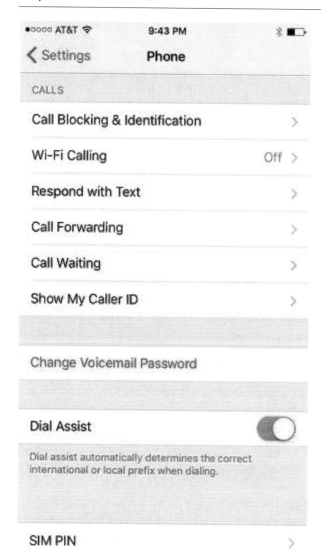

Figure 2: Phone Settings Screen

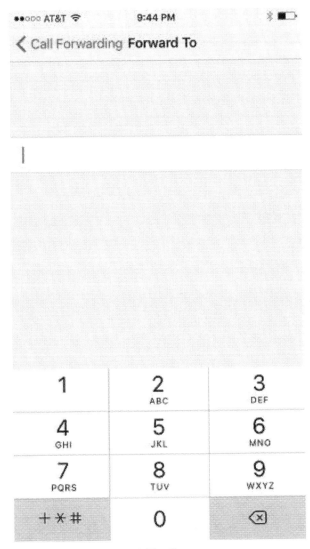

Figure 3: Forward To Screen

2. Turning Call Waiting On or Off

While you are on the line with someone, the Call Waiting feature allows the iPhone to alert you when there is a second incoming call. To turn Call Waiting on or off:

1. Touch the ⚙ icon. The Settings screen appears.
2. Scroll down and touch **Phone**. The Phone Settings screen appears.
3. Touch **Call Waiting**. The Call Waiting screen appears, as shown in **Figure 4**.

4. Touch the  switch next to 'Call Waiting'. The switch appears and Call Waiting is turned off. To turn off Call Waiting, touch the switch next to 'Call Waiting'.

Figure 4: Call Waiting Screen

3. Turning Caller ID On or Off

The Caller ID feature shows your phone number or name (if your number is stored in the recipient's Phonebook) on the called party's device. In order to preserve privacy and make your phone number appear as "Private Number", turn the Caller ID feature off. To turn Caller ID on or off:

1. Touch the ⚙ icon. The Settings screen appears.
2. Scroll down and touch **Phone**. The Phone Settings screen appears.
3. Touch **Show My Caller ID**. The Show My Caller ID screen appears, as shown in **Figure 5**.
4. Touch the ⬤ switch next to 'Show My Caller ID'. The ◯ switch appears and Caller ID is turned off. To turn off Caller ID, touch the ◯ switch next to 'Show My Caller ID'.

Note: When Caller ID is turned off, even those who have your phone number stored in their Phonebook will not be able to view your number when receiving a call from you.

Figure 5: Show My Caller ID Screen

4. Turning the International Assist On or Off

The International Assist feature is useful while traveling abroad. This feature will automatically add the correct international prefix to every phone number that you dial when calling a U.S. phone number. To turn International Assist on or off:

1. Touch the ⊚ icon. The Settings screen appears.
2. Scroll down and touch **Phone**. The Phone Settings screen appears.
3. Touch the ⊸ switch next to 'Dial Assist'. The ⊶ switch appears and International Assist is turned on. To turn off Dial Assist, touch the ⊶ switch next to 'Dial Assist'.

Note: The International Assist feature does not work in all areas.

5. Blocking Specific Numbers

The device can block contacts with specified numbers from calling or texting you. In order to block a number, you must first add it to your Phonebook. To specify numbers to block:

1. Touch the ⊚ icon. The Settings screen appears.
2. Scroll down and touch **Phone**. The Phone Settings screen appears.
3. Touch **Call Blocking & Identification**. The Call Blocking & Identification screen appears, as shown in **Figure 6**.
4. Touch **Block Contact**. Your Phonebook appears.
5. Touch a contact. The contact's number is added to the Blocked list.

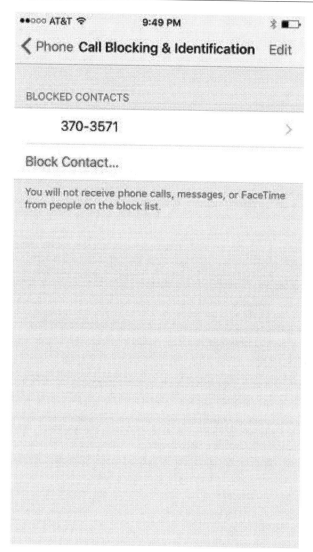

Figure 6: Call Blocking & Identification Screen

6. Editing Preset Text Message Responses

The device allows you to respond with a preset text if you are unable to answer a call. To edit the preset text message responses:

1. Touch the 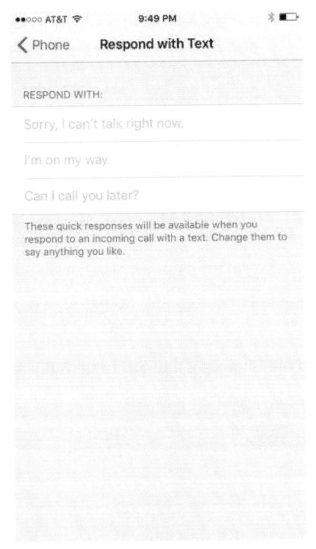 icon. The Settings screen appears.
2. Scroll down and touch **Phone**. The Phone Settings screen appears.
3. Touch **Respond with Text**. The Respond with Text screen appears, as shown in **Figure 7**.
4. Touch one of the messages under 'Respond With" to edit it.
5. Touch **Phone** at the top of the screen. The new preset text messages are saved.

Figure 7: Respond with Text Screen

Adjusting Text Message Settings

Table of Contents

1. Turning iMessage On or Off
2. Turning Read Receipts On or Off in iMessage
3. Turning 'Send as SMS' On or Off (iPhone Only)
4. Turning MMS Messaging On or Off (iPhone Only)
5. Turning the Subject Field On or Off
6. Turning the Character Count On or Off (iPhone Only)
7. Turning Group Messaging On or Off (iPhone Only)
8. Setting the Amount of Time to Keep Messages
9. Setting the Expiration Time for Audio Messages
10. Turning Raise to Listen On or Off (iPhone Only)
11. Blocking Unknown Senders

1. Turning iMessage On or Off

The iMessage feature allows you to send free text messages to iPhone, iPad, or iPod Touch. Turn on iMessage to send a message to another device, or to an iPad or iPod touch, using the email address assigned to the recipient's iMessage account. By default, iMessage is turned on. You cannot send a text message using the iPad or iPod Touch without turning on iMessage. When iMessage is turned off on the iPhone and you send a text message to another device, standard text messaging rates apply as set forth by your network provider. To turn iMessage on or off:

1. Touch the ⊚ icon. The Settings screen appears, as shown in **Figure 1**.
2. Scroll down and touch **Messages**. The Message Settings screen appears, as shown in **Figure 2**.

3. Touch the ⬯ switch next to 'iMessage'. The ⬮ switch appears and iMessage is turned on. To turn off iMessage, touch the ⬮ switch next to 'iMessage'.

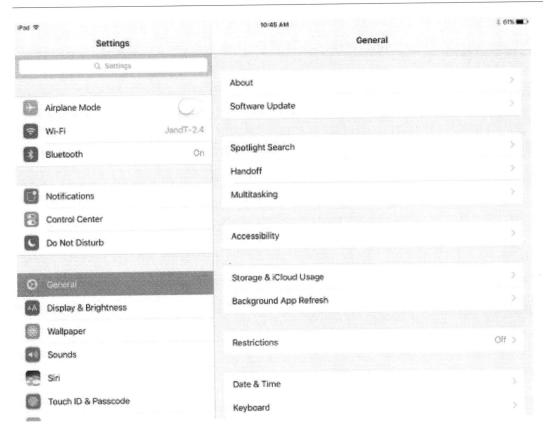

Figure 1: Settings Screen

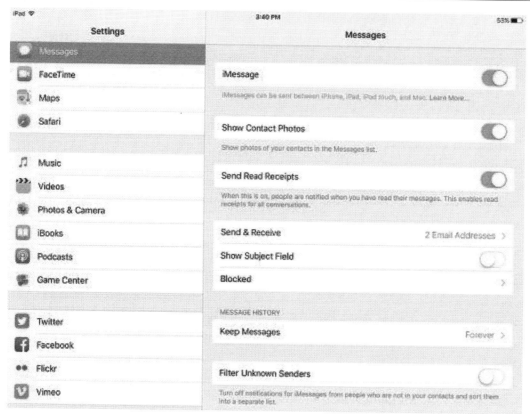

Figure 2: Message Settings Screen

2. Turning Read Receipts On or Off in iMessage

After receiving and opening a message from an iPhone, iPad, or iPod Touch, your device can notify the sender that you have opened and read the message. These notifications are called Read Receipts, and appear under the original message on the sender's screen as "Read", followed by a time. Read Receipts are only compatible with the three Apple devices listed above. To turn Read Receipts on or off:

1. Touch the ⚙ icon. The Settings screen appears.
2. Scroll down and touch **Messages**. The Message Settings screen appears.
3. Touch the ⬜ switch next to 'Send Read Receipts'. The 🔵 switch appears and Read Receipts are turned on. To turn off Read Receipts, touch the 🔵 switch next to 'Send Read Receipts'.

3. Turning 'Send as SMS' On or Off (iPhone Only)

When a message cannot be sent via iMessage, your iPhone can attempt to send it as a regular text message, also known as an SMS. To turn Send as SMS on or off:

1. Touch the ⚙ icon. The Settings screen appears.
2. Scroll down and touch **Messages**. The Message Settings screen appears.

3. Touch the ⬤ switch next to 'Send as SMS'. The ⬤ switch appears and 'Send as SMS' is turned on. To turn off Send as SMS, touch the ⬤ switch next to 'Send as SMS'.

Note: When 'Send as SMS' is turned off, you will only be able to send a message to an device, iPad, or iPod, which has iMessage enabled.

4. Turning MMS Messaging On or Off (iPhone Only)

When you are running low on data, it can be useful to disable MMS messaging, also known as media messaging, to avoid receiving unwanted picture messages that will use up the data too quickly. To turn MMS messaging on or off:

1. Touch the ⚙ icon. The Settings screen appears.
2. Scroll down and touch **Messages**. The Message Settings screen appears.

3. Touch the ⬤ switch next to 'MMS Messaging'. The ⬤ switch appears and MMS Messaging is turned off. To turn off MMS Messaging, touch the ⬤ switch next to 'MMS Messaging'.

5. Turning the Subject Field On or Off

The iPhone can attach a subject to each text message it sends when the subject field is enabled. On most phones, the subject will appear in parentheses preceding the message content. To turn the subject field on or off:

1. Touch the ⚙ icon. The Settings screen appears.
2. Scroll down and touch **Messages**. The Message Settings screen appears.

3. Touch the ⬜ switch next to 'Show Subject Field'. The ⬜ switch appears and the Subject field is turned on. To turn off Show Subject Field, touch the ⬜ switch next to 'Show Subject Field'.

---

6. Turning the Character Count On or Off (iPhone Only)

The Messaging application can show you the number of characters that you have typed when entering a message. To turn the character count on or off:

1. Touch the ⚙ icon. The Settings screen appears.
2. Scroll down and touch **Messages**. The Message Settings screen appears.
3. Touch the ⬜ switch next to 'Character Count'. The ⬜ switch appears and the Character Count is turned on. To turn off Character Count, touch the ⬜ switch next to 'Character Count'.

---

7. Turning Group Messaging On or Off (iPhone Only)

When sending a text message, responses from any of the recipients are sent to everyone that you originally messaged. This feature is known as Group Messaging. To turn Group Messaging on or off:

1. Touch the ⚙ icon. The Settings screen appears.
2. Scroll down and touch **Messages**. The Message Settings screen appears.
3. Touch the ⬜ switch next to 'Group Messaging'. The ⬜ switch appears and the Group Messaging is turned on. To turn off Group Messaging, touch the ⬜ switch next to 'Group Messaging'.

8. Setting the Amount of Time to Keep Messages

When using iMessage, text messages can be automatically deleted after a certain period of time. To set the amount of time to keep messages:

1. Touch the ⚙ icon. The Settings screen appears.
2. Scroll down and touch **Messages**. The Message Settings screen appears.
3. Touch **Keep Messages**. The Keep Messages screen appears, as shown in **Figure 3**.
4. Touch **30 Days** or **1 Year** to select the amount of time, or touch **Forever** to prevent the device from erasing any messages.

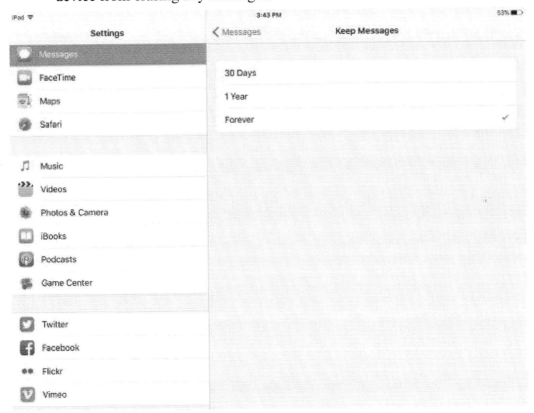

Figure 3: Keep Messages Screen

9. Setting the Expiration Time for Audio Messages

When an audio message is sent using iMessage, it can be set to expire after two minutes, at which point it is removed from your device. Refer to *"Adding a Voice Message to a Conversation (iMessage Only)"* on page 104 to learn how to attach audio messages in iMessage. To set the expiration time for audio messages:

1. Touch the ⬤ icon. The Settings screen appears.
2. Scroll down and touch **Messages**. The Message Settings screen appears.
3. Touch **Expire** under 'Audio Messages'. The Audio Message Expiration screen appears, as shown in **Figure 4**.
4. Touch **After 2 Minutes**, or touch **Never** to keep audio messages.

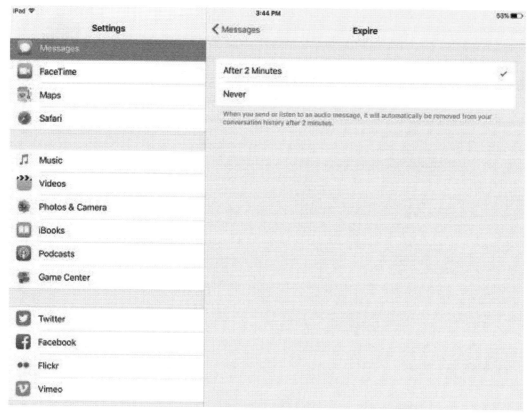

Figure 4: Audio Message Expiration Screen

10. Turning Raise to Listen On or Off (iPhone Only)

The Raise to Listen feature allows you to raise the iPhone to your ear to listen to audio messages. To turn Raise to Listen on or off:

1. Touch the ⚙ icon. The Settings screen appears.
2. Scroll down and touch **Messages**. The Message Settings screen appears.
3. Touch the ⬜ switch next to 'Raise to Listen'. The 🔵 switch appears and the Raise to Listen is turned on. To turn off Raise to Listen, touch the 🔵 switch next to 'Raise to Listen'.

11. Blocking Unknown Senders

You can prevent numbers that you do not know from messaging you. In order to block a number, you must first add it to your Phonebook. To specify numbers to block:

1. Touch the ⚙ icon. The Settings screen appears.
2. Scroll down and touch **Messages**. The Message Settings screen appears.
3. Touch **Blocked**. The Blocked screen appears, as shown in **Figure 5**.
4. Touch **Add New**. Your Phonebook appears.
5. Touch a contact. The contact's number is added to the Blocked list.

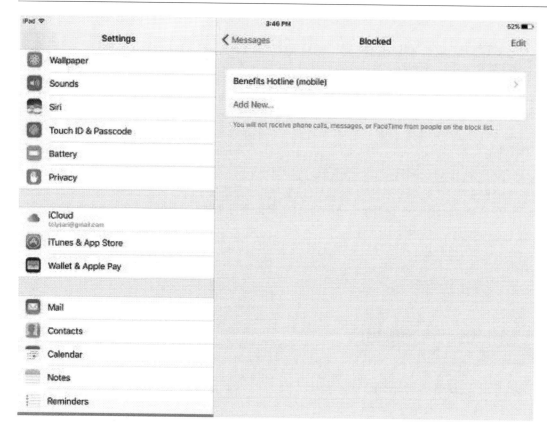

Figure 5: Blocked Screen

Tips and Tricks

Table of Contents

1. Maximizing Battery Life
2. Taking a Screenshot
3. Scrolling to the Top of a Screen
4. Saving an Image While Browsing the Internet
5. Inserting a Period
6. Adding an Extension to a Contact's Number (iPhone only)
7. Navigating the Home Screens
8. Typing Alternate Characters
9. Quickly Deleting Recently Typed Text
10. Resetting the Device
11. Calling a Phone Number on a Website
12. Taking Notes
13. Recovering Signal After Being in an Area with No Service
14. Changing the Number of Rings Before the Device Goes to Voicemail (iPhone only)
15. Deleting a Song in the Music Application
16. Taking a Picture from the Lock Screen
17. Assigning a Custom Ringtone to a Contact
18. Opening the Photos Application without Closing the Camera
19. Inserting Emoticons
20. Hiding the Keyboard in the Messages Application
21. Controlling Web Surfing Using Gestures
22. Navigating the Menus Using Gestures
23. Pausing or Cancelling an Application Download
24. Making a Quick Note for a Contact
25. Using a Search Engine that Does Not Track Your Searches
26. Preventing Applications from Refreshing in the Background
27. Leaving Your Home Screen Free of Icons
28. Call Waiting in FaceTime
29. Viewing Battery Usage
30. Attaching Any File Type to an Email
31. Viewing Favorite Contacts Using 3D Touch
32. Moving the Text Cursor Like a Computer Mouse
33. Saving Data by Sending Smaller Pictures
34. Filtering Email to Customize Your Inbox
35. Using 3D Touch in the Control Center (iPhone 6S and Later Only)

1. Maximizing Battery Life

There are several things you can do to increase the battery life of the device.

- Lock the device whenever you are not using it. To lock the device, press the **Sleep/Wake** button at the top of the device. Refer to *"Button Layout"* on page 23 for the location of the Sleep/Wake button.
- Keep the Auto-lock feature on and set it to a small amount of time. Refer to *"Changing Auto-Lock Settings"* on page 247 to learn how to change Auto-lock settings.
- Turn down the brightness and turn off Auto-Brightness. Refer to *"Adjusting the Brightness"* on page 249 to learn how.
- urn on Airplane mode in areas where there is little or no signal, as the device will continually try to search for service. Refer to *"Turning Airplane Mode On or Off"* on page 215 to learn how to turn on Airplane Mode. This tip is for iPhone and iPad 4G only.
- Make sure to let the battery drain completely and then charge it fully at least once a month. This will help both short-term and long-term battery life.
- Turn off Wi-Fi when it is not in use. Refer to *"Using Wi-Fi"* on page 40 to learn how.
- Turn off Location Services when it is not in use. Refer to *"Turning Location Services On or Off"* on page 216 to learn how.
- Turn on the Grayscale accessibility feature. This will prevent you from seeing any colors, but is a great feature to use when your battery is running low. Refer to *"Managing Vision Accessibility Features"* on page 267 to learn how.

You can view a list of applications that are using up most of your battery. To view battery usage, touch the icon, and then touch **Battery**. The Battery screen appears, showing all of the applications that are draining your battery, and the percentage of the battery that each has drained. Refer to *"Closing an Application Running in the Background"* on page 199 to learn how to cut down on the amount of battery used by applications. You can also turn on Low Power Mode from this screen. Low Power Mode reduces the performance, but increases the battery life of your device.

2. Taking a Screenshot

To capture what is on the screen and save it as a photo, press and hold the **Home** button, and then press the **Sleep/Wake** Button. Release the buttons and the screen will momentarily flash white. The screenshot is saved to the 'Screenshots' album.

3. Scrolling to the Top of a Screen

Touch anywhere in the notification bar at the very top of the screen to quickly scroll to the top of a list, website, etc. The notification bar is where the clock and battery meter are located.

4. Saving an Image While Browsing the Internet

To save an image from Safari to the device, touch and hold the picture until the Image menu appears. Touch **Save Image**. The image is saved to the 'Recently Added' album.

5. Inserting a Period

When typing a sentence, touch the space bar twice quickly to insert a period and a space.

6. Adding an Extension to a Contact's Number (iPhone only)

When entering a number for a stored contact, you can add an extension that will be dialed following a short pause after the call is connected. While entering a number, touch the ＋ ✳ ＃ button in the lower left-hand corner of the screen, and then touch **Pause**. A comma appears, and you can now enter an extension. Each comma represents one second that the phone will wait after dialing the number.

7. Navigating the Home Screens

Typically, you navigate to another Home screen by touching the screen and sliding your finger to the left or right. Alternatively, touch one of the gray dots at the bottom of a Home screen to go to the previous or next screen.

8. Typing Alternate Characters

When typing a sentence, insert other characters, such as Á or Ñ, by touching and holding the base letter. A menu of characters appears above the letter. Slide your finger to a character to insert it.

9. Quickly Deleting Recently Typed Text

This feature is quite a secret. If you have just typed several lines of text and do not want any of it, just give the device a good shake. A menu appears asking whether to undo the typing. Touch **Undo**. The typed text is erased. Give the device another shake to redo the typing. This works in any application, or while text messaging.

10. Resetting the Device

If the device or an application freezes up or is acting strangely, you may wish to reset the device. This will NOT wipe any data, but simply restart the operating system. To reset the device, hold the **Home** button and **Sleep/Wake** button together until the device completely shuts off. Continue to hold the buttons until the logo appears. The device resets and starts up.

11. Calling a Phone Number on a Website

You can call a phone number on a website directly. The number will be blue and underlined, much like a link. Touch the number. The device calls it. If the number is on a website, the device will ask whether to call the number. Touch **Call**. This may not work with all websites.

12. Taking Notes

A convenient way to take notes is by using the built-in Notes application and emailing the notes to yourself. To take notes, touch the icon on the Home screen. Touch **New** at the top of the screen to add a note. Touch the icon at the bottom of the screen and then touch **Mail** to email the note.

13. Recovering Signal After Being in an Area with No Service

Sometimes the device has trouble finding signal after returning from an area where your network was not available. This issue can sometimes be fixed by turning Airplane Mode on and then back off. Refer to *"Turning Airplane Mode On or Off"* on page 215 to learn how.

14. Changing the Number of Rings Before the Device Goes to Voicemail (iPhone only)

There is a hidden way to change the number of times the device rings before going to Voicemail. The maximum number of seconds the phone can ring is 30. Have a pen and paper ready, as you will need to enter a long number. To change the number of times the device rings before going to Voicemail:

1. Turn off Call Forwarding. Refer to *"Turning Call Forwarding On or Off"* on page 274 to learn how.
2. Touch the ☎ icon and then touch the ☷ icon. The Keypad appears.
3. Dial ***#61#** exactly as it appears here and touch **CALL**. When the call is completed, the Voicemail Configuration screen appears.
4. Write down the number that follows "Forwards to." Skip the '+' since you will be typing it in later anyway.
5. Touch **Dismiss**. The call is ended.
6. Dial ***61*+XXXXXXXXXX*11*tt#** exactly as it appears here, where the X's represent the number you just wrote down and "tt" is the number of seconds you want for the device to ring before going to Voicemail. For example, if the number you wrote down is 1234567890 and the number of seconds you prefer is 30, you would dial *61*+11234567890*11*30#. To make the plus sign appear when dialing a phone number, touch and hold **0**.
7. Touch **CALL.** The number of seconds the device rings is changed and a confirmation appears.
8. Touch **Dismiss**. The call is ended.

Note: To change the ring time back, just repeat these steps. The number you wrote down in step three does not change, so you can proceed to step four if you know it. The default ring time for the device is 20 seconds.

15. Deleting a Song in the Music Application

To delete a song from your device, touch the ••• button next to a song, and touch **Remove**. A confirmation appears. Touch **Remove Download** or **Delete from Library**. If you selected **Remove Download**, you can still stream the song from iCloud, but it does not take up space on your device. If you selected **Delete from Library**, the song is hidden both in iCloud and on your device. Deleting songs from the library is not recommended because restoring (unhiding) them involves a complicated process. Refer to the instructions below to learn how to unhide a deleted song.

Note: If you do not see the ••• *button, touch the album cover in the bottom right-hand corner of the screen.*

To unhide a song in your library:

1. Open iTunes on your computer.
2. Click **Account** or click your name at the top of the window.
3. Click **Account Info** or **View My Account**. The Account Information screen appears.
4. Scroll down to the iTunes in the Cloud section, then click **Manage** next to Hidden Purchases. From this screen, you can unhide songs and albums.

16. Taking a Picture from the Lock Screen

To take a picture without unlocking the device, slide your finger to the left. The camera turns on. Press the **Volume Up** button. The camera takes a picture.

17. Assigning a Custom Ringtone to a Contact

You can assign a custom ringtone to any contact in the Phonebook. To assign a ringtone to a contact:

1. Touch the ▨ icon. The Phonebook appears.
2. Find and touch the contact to whom you wish to assign a custom ringtone. The Contact Info screen appears. Refer to *"Finding a Contact"* on page 70 to learn more.
3. Touch **Edit** in the upper right-hand corner of the screen. The Contact Editing screen appears.

4. Touch **Ringtone**. A list of available ringtones appears.
5. Touch a ringtone. The ringtone plays.
6. Touch **Done**. The ringtone is assigned to the contact.

Note: Refer to "Buying Music and Ringtones in iTunes" *on page 152 to learn how to purchase additional ringtones.*

18. Opening the Photos Application without Closing the Camera

To open the Photos application while the camera is turned on, touch the photo thumbnail next to the ⬜ button. To return to the camera, touch **Camera** in the upper left-hand corner.

19. Inserting Emoticons

The Emoji keyboard contains over 460 new emoticons that can be used when entering text. To learn how to add the Emoji keyboard, refer to *"Adding an International Keyboard"* on page 237, and touch **Emoji** in step 6. After adding the Emoji keyboard, touch the 😊 key, if the Emoji keyboard is the only one that you have added, or touch the 🌐 key if there are other keyboards in addition to English and Emoji. The Emoji keyboard appears. If you touched the 🌐 key, you may need to touch it again to cycle through the keyboards until the Emoji keyboard turns on.

20. Hiding the Keyboard in the Messages Application

While reading a text message, you can hide the keyboard to view more of the conversation at once. Touch the last visible message in the conversation and slide your finger down to the keyboard. The keyboard is hidden.

21. Controlling Web Surfing Using Gestures

Instead of touching the ⟨ and ⟩ buttons to go back and forward, respectively, you can touch the right or left edge of the screen and slide your finger to the left or right, respectively.

22. Navigating the Menus Using Gestures

Instead of touching the text in the upper left-hand corner of the screen to return to the previous menu, just touch the left-hand side of the screen and slide your finger to the right. This works in most applications as well, such as the Music application.

23. Pausing or Cancelling an Application Download

If you are downloading more than one application at a time, you may wish to pause one of the downloads so that one of the other applications downloads first. To pause an application download, touch the application icon of the application that you wish to pause. Touch the icon again to resume the download. You may also cancel the download by deleting the application. Refer to *"Deleting an Application"* on page 200 to learn how.

Note: If you cancel a download by deleting the application, you will still be charged if the application was not free. You may still download the application later. Refer to "Buying an Application" *on page 196 to learn how.*

24. Making a Quick Note for a Contact

You may take a quick note for a contact without having to edit the entire contents of the contact. To make a quick note for a contact, touch **Notes** on the contact's information screen. Touch **All Contacts** at the top of the screen to save the note.

25. Using a Search Engine that Does Not Track Your Searches

Safari now allows you to use a new search engine, called DuckDuckGo. This search engine comes from a start-up company, and allows you to search the Web without tracking your searches like Google. Refer to *"Changing the Search Engine"* on page 122 to learn how to change your search engine to DuckDuckGo.

26. Preventing Applications from Refreshing in the Background

Certain applications, such as Podcasts and Weather will refresh their content even when the application is closed. This can drain your battery more quickly. To prevent applications from refreshing in the background:

1. Touch the icon. The Settings screen appears.
2. Touch **General**. The General Settings screen appears.
3. Touch **Background App Refresh**. The Background App Refresh screen appears.
4. Touch the switch next to 'Background App Refresh'. The switch appears and the feature is turned off.

27. Leaving Your Home Screen Free of Icons

If you are a wallpaper connoisseur, you may wish to leave your main Home screen empty. In iOS 7 and earlier, if you tried to move all of your icons to other screens, the second Home screen took the place of the first. As of iOS 8, you may move all of your icons to other screens, and leave your main Home screen empty. This way, you can look at your wallpaper all day long without the intrusion of those pesky icons.

28. Call Waiting in FaceTime

FaceTime now allows you to accept another call while you are already on a call. To accept a call and end the current one, touch **End & Accept**. To reject an incoming call, touch **Decline**.

29. Viewing Battery Usage

If your battery is dying too quickly or if you are curious how your battery is being used, you can check the percentage of your battery that is used by each application. To view the battery usage, touch the [icon] icon. The Settings screen appears. Touch **Battery**. The Battery screen appears. Check the Battery Usage section to determine how your battery is being used.

30. Attaching Any File Type to an Email

In addition to attaching photos and videos to an email, you can attach other files, such as those that are in your iCloud or Google Drive. To attach a file to an email when using an iPad, touch the [icon] button, which is located above the [icon] key. On an iPhone, touch and hold text in the email, then touch **Add Attachment** from the Text menu.

31. Viewing Favorite Contacts Using 3D Touch

To quickly view your Favorites, use 3D Touch (firmly press) the [icon] icon. The list of your Favorites appears.

32. Moving the Text Cursor Like a Computer Mouse

Whenever you use the virtual keyboard, you can move the text cursor freely as if you are using a mouse. Use 3D Touch (firmly press) the screen and move your finger in any direction.

33. Saving Data by Sending Smaller Pictures

You can conserve your data by reducing the size and quality of photos when you send them via text message. To reduce photo size and quality in text messages:

1. Touch the [icon] icon. The Settings screen appears.
2. Touch **Messages**. The Messages settings screen appears.

3. Touch the ⬭ switch next to 'Low Quality Image Mode'. The feature is turned on. To turn off the feature, touch the ⬤ switch.

34. Filtering Email to Customize Your Inbox

By default, the Mail application sorts your email by date, with the most recent emails at the top. Although you can search your email, sometimes you do not know precisely what you're trying to find. You can filter your email to easily find specific emails, such as those that are unread, flagged, or which contain attachments. To filter email, touch the ⊜ button in the bottom left-hand corner of the screen. Then, touch **Filtered by** and select as many filters as you need. Touch **Done** to filter your email.

35. Using 3D Touch in the Control Center (iPhone 6S and Later Only)

You can use 3D Touch in the Control Center to access additional features. 3D Touch (firmly press) one of the following icons to perform the corresponding action:

- Change the brightness of the flashlight.

- Set a quick timer for one, five, 20, or 60 minutes.

- Copy the last result of a calculation.

- Quickly capture a photo, selfie, video, or slo-mo.

Troubleshooting

Table of Contents

1. Device does not turn on
2. Device is not responding
3. Can't make a call (iPhone only)
4. Can't surf the web
5. Screen or keyboard does not rotate
6. iTunes does not detect device when connected to a computer
7. Device does not ring or play music, can't hear while talking, can't listen to voicemails
8. Low microphone volume, caller can't hear you (iPhone only)
9. Camera does not work
10. Device shows the White Screen of Death
11. "DEVICE needs to cool down" message appears
12. Display does not adjust brightness automatically

1. Device does not turn on

If the device does not power on, try one or more of the following tips:

- **Recharge the device** - Use the included wall charger to charge the battery. If the battery power is extremely low, the screen will not turn on for several minutes. Do NOT use the USB port on your computer to charge the device.
- **Replace the battery** - If you purchased the device a long time ago, you may need to replace the battery. Contact Apple to learn how.
- **Reset the device** - This method will not erase any data. Hold down the **Home** button and **Sleep/Wake** button at the same time for 10 seconds. Keep holding the two buttons until the logo appears and the device restarts.

2. Device is not responding

If the device is frozen or is not responding, try one or more of the following. These steps solve most problems on the device.

- **Exit the application** - If the device freezes while running an application, hold the **Home** Button for six seconds. The application quits and the device returns to the Home screen.
- **Turn the device off and then back on** - If the device is still frozen, try pressing the **Sleep/Wake** button to turn the device off. Keep holding the **Sleep/Wake** Button until "Slide to Power Off" appears. Slide your finger from left to right over the text. The device turns off. After the screen is completely black, press the **Sleep/Wake** button again to turn the device back on.
- **Restart the device** - Hold the **Home** button and **Sleep/Wake** button at the same time for 10 seconds or until the ⌘ logo appears.
- **Remove Media** - Some downloaded applications or music may freeze up the device. Try deleting some of the media that may be problematic after restarting the device. Refer to *"Deleting an Application"* on page 200 to learn how to delete an application. You may also erase all data at once by doing the following:

Warning: Once erased, data cannot be recovered. Make sure you back up any files you wish to keep.

1. Touch the ⊚ icon. The Settings screen appears.
2. Touch **General**. The General Settings screen appears.
3. Touch **Reset**. The Reset screen appears.
4. Touch **Erase All Content and Settings**. A confirmation dialog appears.
5. Touch **Erase**. The device is restored to factory settings.

3. Can't make a call (iPhone Only)

If the device cannot make outgoing calls, try one of the following:

- If "No Service" is shown at the top of the screen, the network does not cover you in your location. Try moving to a different location, or even to a different part of a building.
- Try walking around to find more signal.

- Turn off Airplane Mode if you have it turned on. If that does not work, try turning Airplane Mode on for 15 seconds and then turning it off. Refer to **Turning Airplane Mode On or Off** to learn how.
- Make sure you dialed an area code with the phone number.
- Turn the device off and back on.

4. Can't surf the web

If you have no internet access, there may be little or no service in your area. Try moving to a different location or turning on Wi-Fi, if available. Refer to **Using Wi-Fi** to learn how to turn on Wi-Fi. If you still cannot access the Web, refer to *"Device is not responding"* on page 305 for further assistance.

5. Screen or keyboard does not rotate

If the screen does not rotate, or the full, horizontal keyboard does not appear when you rotate the device, it may be one of these issues:

- The application does not support the horizontal view.
- The device is lying flat. Hold the device upright to change the view in applications that support it.

- The rotation lock is on. The rotation is locked if the icon appears next to the battery life at the top of the screen. Touch the bottom of the screen and slide your finger up to access the Control Center. In the control center, touch the icon to unlock the rotation. On an iPad, if you do not see the icon in the Control Center, then the rotation can be controlled using the Side switch above the Volume Controls.

6. iTunes does not detect device when connected to a computer

If iTunes does not detect the device when connecting it to your computer, try using a different USB port. If that does not work, turn the device off and on again while it is plugged in to the computer. If the device indicates that it is connected, the problem might be with your computer. Try restarting your computer or reinstalling iTunes. Otherwise, refer to *"Device is not responding"* on page 305 for assistance.

7. Device does not ring or play music, can't hear while talking, can't listen to voicemails

Make sure the volume is turned up. Refer to *"Button Layout"* on page 23 to find the Volume Controls. Check whether you can still hear sound through headphones. The headphone jack is located on the top of the device. If you can hear sound through headphones, try inserting the headphones and taking them out several times. Sometimes the sensor in the headphone jack malfunctions.

8. Low microphone volume, caller can't hear you (iPhone only)

If you are talking to someone who can't hear you, try the following:

- Take off any cases or other accessories as these may cover up the microphone.
- When you first take the device out of the box, it comes with a piece of plastic covering the microphone. Make sure to take this plastic off before using the device.
- If the caller cannot hear you at all, you may have accidentally muted the conversation. Refer to *"Using the Mute Function During a Voice Call"* on page 63 to learn how turn Mute on or off.

9. Camera does not work

If the device camera is not functioning correctly, try one of the following:
- Clean the camera lens with a polishing cloth.
- Take off any cases or accessories that may interfere with the camera lens on the back of the device.

- Hold the device steady when taking a picture. A shaky hand often results in a blurry picture. Try leaning against a stationary object to stabilize your hand.

- If you cannot find the [camera icon] icon on your Home screen, try the following:

1. Touch the [settings icon] icon. The Settings screen appears.
2. Touch **General**. The General Settings screen appears.
3. Touch **Restrictions**. The Restrictions screen appears.
4. Touch **Disable Restrictions**. The Restrictions Passcode screen appears.
5. Enter the passcode that you set up when you enabled the restrictions. All restrictions are disabled.

10. Device shows the White Screen of Death

If the device screen has gone completely white, try restarting or restoring the device. Refer to *"Device is not responding"* on page 305 to learn how.

11. "DEVICE needs to cool down" message appears

If you leave the device in your car on a hot day, or expose it to direct sunlight for too long, one of the following may happen:

- Device stops charging
- Weak signal
- Screen dims
- Device breaks completely
- "DEVICE needs to cool down" message appears, where DEVICE refers to the type of iOS 10 device that you have.

Before using the device, allow it to cool. The device works best in temperatures between 32°F and 95°F (0°C to 35°C). While it is turned off, store the device at temperatures between -4°F and 113°F (-20°C to 45°C).

12. Display does not adjust brightness automatically

If the device does not brighten in bright conditions, or does not become dimmer in dark conditions, try taking any cases or accessories off. A case may block the light sensor, located at the top of the device. Also, check to make sure that Auto-Brightness is turned on. Refer to *"Adjusting the Brightness"* on page 249 to learn how to turn on Auto-Brightness.

Index

A

Accessing Quick Settings through the Control Center, 44
Adding a Bookmark to the Home Screen, 118
Adding a Keyboard Shortcut, 239
Adding a New Contact, 69
Adding a Voice Message to a Conversation (iMessage Only), 104
Adding an Extension to a Contact's Number (iPhone only), 296
Adding an International Keyboard, 237
Adding and Viewing Bookmarks, 115
Adding Texted Phone Numbers to the Phonebook, 97
Adjusting Accessibility Settings, 267
Adjusting General Settings, 247
Adjusting Language and Keyboard Settings, 235
Adjusting Live Photos (iPhone 6S and Later Only), 20
Adjusting Phone Settings (iPhone Only), 274
Adjusting Siri Settings, 234
Adjusting Sound Settings, 227
Adjusting Text Message Settings, 285
Adjusting the Brightness, 249
Adjusting Wireless Settings, 215
Application-Specific Phrases for Siri, 214
Archiving Emails, 183
Assigning a Custom Ringtone to a Contact, 299
Assigning a Passcode Lock or Fingerprint Lock, 251
Attaching a Picture or Video to an Email, 178
Attaching Any File Type to an Email, 303

B

Blocking Pop-Up Windows, 121
Blocking Specific Numbers, 281
Blocking Unknown Senders, 292
Browsing Photos, 133
Browsing Photos by Date and Location, 143
Button Layout, 23
Buying an Application, 196
Buying Music and Ringtones in iTunes, 152
Buying or Renting Videos in iTunes, 153

C

Call Waiting in FaceTime, 302
Calling a Contact, 53
Calling a Favorite, 55
Calling a Phone Number on a Website, 297
Calling the Sender from within a Text (iPhone Only), 94

Camera does not work, 308
Can't make a call (iPhone Only), 306
Can't surf the web, 307
Capturing a Video, 131
Capturing and Viewing a Live Photo (iPhone 6S and Later Only), 150
Changing Application Settings, 199
Changing Auto-Lock Settings, 247
Changing Email Options, 185
Changing the Contact Sort Order, 77
Changing the Default Signature, 184
Changing the Keyboard Layout, 243
Changing the Number of Rings Before the Device Goes to Voicemail (iPhone only), 298
Changing the Operating System Language, 241
Changing the Region Format, 245
Changing the Search Engine, 122
Changing the Wallpaper, 261
Charging the Device, 27
Checking the Time and Setting Alarms Using Siri, 211
Clearing the History and Browsing Data, 123
Closing an Application Running in the Background, 199
Composing a New Text Message, 81
Controlling Siri's Voice, 232
Controlling Web Surfing Using Gestures, 301
Copying, Cutting, and Pasting Text, 85
Correcting Siri Queries, 19
Creating a Photo Album, 139
Creating a Playlist, 162
Creating an Icon Folder, 39
Customizing Cellular Data Usage (iPhone and iPad 4G only), 218
Customizing Notification and Alert Sounds, 231
Customizing Spelling and Grammar Settings, 235
Customizing the Smart Search Field, 127

D

Deleting a Contact, 72
Deleting a Photo, 138
Deleting a Photo Album, 142
Deleting a Song in the Music Application, 299
Deleting a Text Message, 96
Deleting an Application, 200
Device does not ring or play music, can't hear while talking, can't listen to voicemails, 308
Device does not turn on, 305
Device is not responding, 306
"DEVICE needs to cool down" message appears, 309

Device shows the White Screen of Death, 309
Dialing a Number, 52
Display does not adjust brightness automatically, 310
Downloading Media, 158

E

Editing a Photo, 134
Editing a Photo Album, 140
Editing Contact Information, 73
Editing iTunes Account Information, 191
Editing Preset Text Message Responses, 283
Erasing and Restoring the Device, 259

F

Filtering Email to Customize Your Inbox, 304
Finding a Contact, 70
Flagging an Important Email, 182
Focusing on a Part of the Screen, 133
Formatting Text, 175
Forwarding a Text Message, 92

G

Getting Directions and Finding Businesses Using Siri, 212
Getting Started, 22

H

Handwriting a Message, 110
Hiding the Keyboard in the Messages Application, 300

I

Inserting a Period, 296
Inserting Emoticons, 300
Installing a SIM Card (iPhone and iPad 4G models only), 28
Is My Device Compatible with iOS 10?, 22
iTunes does not detect device when connected to a computer, 308

L

Leaving a Group Conversation, 103
Leaving Your Home Screen Free of Icons, 302
Looking Up Words in the Dictionary Using Siri, 214
Low microphone volume, caller can't hear you (iPhone only), 308

M

Making a Call, 209
Making a Call Over Wi-Fi, 64
Making a Quick Note for a Contact, 301
Making Voice and Video Calls, 52
Managing and Using Widgets, 48
Managing Applications, 188
Managing Contacts, 69
Managing Hearing Accessibility Features, 270
Managing Memories in Photos, 149
Managing Notification Settings, 259
Managing Open Browser Tabs, 119
Managing People in Photos, 148
Managing Photos and Videos, 130
Managing Physical & Motor Accessibility Features, 272
Managing the Address Book Using Siri, 210
Managing Vision Accessibility Features, 267
Marking Up Photos, 14
Maximizing Battery Life, 295
Moving an Email in the Inbox to Another Folder, 181
Moving the Text Cursor Like a Computer Mouse, 303

N

Naming a Conversation, 104
Navigating the Home Screens, 296
Navigating the Menus Using Gestures, 301
Navigating the Screens, 38
Navigating to a Website, 114

O

Opening the Photos Application without Closing the Camera, 300
Organizing Applications into Folders, 199
Organizing Icons, 39

P

Pausing or Cancelling an Application Download, 301
Pausing, Resuming, or Cancelling a Download Using 3D Touch (iPhone 6S and Later Only), 18
Playing Media, 156
Playing Music, 158
Playing Music Using Siri, 213
Playing Music while Taking Live Photos (iPhone 6S and Later Only), 19
Preventing Applications from Refreshing in the Background, 302
Previewing a Link Image in a Message, 15
Putting a Caller on Hold (hidden button), 63

Q

Quickly Deleting Recently Typed Text, 297

R

Reading a Stored Text Message, 92
Reading Email, 171
Reading Transcriptions of Your Voicemails (iPhone Only), 13
Reading User Reviews, 199
Receiving a Text Message, 88
Receiving a Voice Call, 58
Recording a Time-Lapse Video, 145
Recovering Deleted Photos, 145
Recovering Signal After Being in an Area with No Service, 298
Redeeming a Gifted Application, 203
Referring to Another Email when Composing a New Message, 174
Registering with Apple, 152
Removing System Application Icons, 20
Renaming a Folder Using 3D Touch (iPhone 6S and Later Only), 18
Replying to an Incoming Call with a Text Message, 60
Replying to and Forwarding Email Messages, 177
Resetting All Settings, 258
Resetting the Device, 297
Resetting the Home Screen Layout, 257
Restricting Access to Private Information, 264
Returning a Recent Phone Call, 57

S

Saving an Image While Browsing the Internet, 296
Saving Data by Sending Smaller Pictures, 303
Scanning a Credit Card Using the Device's Camera, 129
Screen or keyboard does not rotate, 307
Scrolling to the Top of a Screen, 296
Searching for a Photo, 144
Searching for an Application to Purchase, 192
Searching for Media in iTunes, 155
Searching the Device for Content, 48
Searching the Device while Using Any Application, 19
Searching the Web and Asking Questions Using Siri, 213
Sending a Digital Touch, 111
Sending a Hidden Text or Photo in a Message (iPhone 6S and Later Only), 16
Sending a Picture Message, 99
Sending an Application as a Gift, 200
Sending and Receiving Email Using Siri, 212
Sending and Receiving Text Messages Using Siri, 210
Setting a Reminder to Return an Incoming Call, 61
Setting the Amount of Time to Keep Messages, 290

Setting the Default Ringtone, 230
Setting the Expiration Time for Audio Messages, 291
Setting Up a Virtual Private Network (VPN), 220
Setting Up and Managing Meetings Using Siri, 211
Setting Up the AutoFill Feature, 126
Setting Up the Device for the First Time, 30
Setting Up the Mail application, 167
Sharing a Contact's Information, 74
Sharing Your iTunes Account with Family, 156
Sharing Your Location in a Conversation, 105
Showing a Notification within a Folder Using 3D Touch (iPhone 6S and Later Only), 19
Signing In to a Different iTunes Account, 190
Signing In to an iTunes Account, 188
Starting a Conference Call (Adding a Call), 63
Starting a Facetime Call, 67
Starting a Slideshow, 142
Switching Accounts in the Mail application, 172
Switching Between Applications, 197

T

Taking a Picture, 130
Taking a Picture from the Lock Screen, 299
Taking Notes, 297
Text Messaging, 81
Troubleshooting, 305
Turning 24-Hour Mode On or Off, 256
Turning Airplane Mode On or Off, 215
Turning Automatic Application Updates On or Off, 204
Turning Bluetooth On or Off, 223
Turning Call Forwarding On or Off, 274
Turning Call Waiting On or Off, 277
Turning Caller ID On or Off, 279
Turning Data Roaming On or Off (iPhone and iPad 4G only), 220
Turning Group Messaging On or Off (iPhone Only), 289
Turning Guided Access On or Off, 271
Turning iMessage On or Off, 285
Turning Keyboard Clicks On or Off, 232
Turning Location Services On or Off, 216
Turning Lock Sounds On or Off, 231
Turning MMS Messaging On or Off (iPhone Only), 288
Turning Night Shift On or Off, 250
Turning Private Browsing On or Off, 125
Turning Raise to Listen On or Off (iPhone Only), 292
Turning Raise to Wake On or Off (iPhone 6S and Later Only), 266
Turning Read Receipts for a Single Conversation On or Off, 112
Turning Read Receipts On or Off in iMessage, 287
Turning 'Send as SMS' On or Off (iPhone Only), 288
Turning the Character Count On or Off (iPhone Only), 289
Turning the Device On and Off, 28
Turning the International Assist On or Off, 281

Turning the Subject Field On or Off, 288

Turning Vibration On or Off (iPhone Only), 227

Turning Volume Button Functionality On or Off, 229

Typing Alternate Characters, 296

Typing in Multiple Languages at Once, 15

U

Unlocking Your iOS 10 Device, 13

Unsubscribing from a Mailing List, 17

Unsubscribing from an Email List, 185

Using 3D Touch in the Control Center (iPhone 6S and Later Only), 304

Using 3D Touch to Share an Application, 18

Using a Search Engine that Does Not Track Your Searches, 302

Using a Video Overlay to Watch a Video (Certain iPad Models Only), 146

Using Additional Audio Controls, 161

Using Facial Recognition in Photos, 13

Using iMessage Applications, 112

Using Interactive Notifications, 51

Using iTunes, 152

Using Keyboard Predictions, 16

Using Side-by-Side in Safari, 14

Using Side-by-Side to Multitask (iPad Air 2 and Later Only), 208

Using Side-by-Side to Multitask with Mail, 16

Using Side-by-Side to Multitask with Music, 17

Using Siri, 209

Using Slide Over to Multitask (Certain iPad Models Only), 204

Using Tapback in a Message, 111

Using the Digital Zoom, 132

Using the Flash (iPhone Only), 132

Using the iTunes Radio, 165

Using the Keypad During a Voice Call, 62

Using the Mail Application, 167

Using the Music Application, 158

Using the Mute Function During a Voice Call, 63

Using the New Control Center, 14

Using the Notification Center, 47

Using the Safari Web Browser, 114

Using the Speakerphone During a Voice Call, 61

Using the Spell Check Feature, 87

Using Wi-Fi, 40

Using Wi-Fi to Download an Application, 197

Using Wi-Fi to Sync Your Device with Your Computer, 225

V

Viewing a Video on a Webpage while Continuing to Browse, 15

Viewing All Attachments in a Conversation, 107

Viewing an Article in Reader Mode, 123

Viewing Battery Usage, 303

Viewing Categories in the App Store, 17

Viewing Emails in Conversation View, 186

Viewing Favorite Contacts Using 3D Touch, 303

Viewing Lyrics in the Music Application, 20

Viewing Recently Closed Tabs, 128

Viewing Related Photos, 14

Viewing Sender Information from within a Text, 96

Viewing Three Panes in the Mail Application (iPad Pro Only), 17

Viewing Widgets on the Home Screen Using 3D Touch (iPhone 6S and Later Only), 18

W

What's New in iOS 10?, 11

Writing an Email, 173

Other Books from the Author of the Help Me Series, Charles Hughes

Help Me! Guide to the iPhone 6S

Help Me! Guide to the iPhone 6

Help Me! Guide to the iPhone 5

Help Me! Guide to the iPad Air 2

Help Me! Guide to the iPad Air

Help Me! Guide to the iPad 2

Help Me! Guide to the Apple Watch

Help Me! Guide to the iPod Touch

Help Me! Guide to the iPad Mini

Help Me! Guide to iOS 9

Help Me! Guide to iOS 8

Help Me! Guide to the Kindle Fire HDX

Help Me! Guide to the Nexus 7

Help Me! Guide to the Galaxy S5

Help Me! Guide to the Galaxy S4

Help Me! Guide to the HTC One

Help Me! Guide to the Kindle Touch

Help Me! Guide to the Samsung Galaxy Note

Help Me! Guide to the Kindle Fire HD 6

Help Me! Guide to the Kindle Fire TV

Made in the USA
San Bernardino, CA
15 December 2017